Also by Mark Bittman

Food Matters: A Guide to Conscious Eating with More Than 75 Recipes

How to Cook Everything

How to Cook Everything Vegetarian

The Best Recipes in the World

Fish: The Complete Guide to Buying and Cooking

How to Cook Everything: The Basics

How to Cook Everything: Bittman Takes On America's Chefs

Mark Bittman's Quick and Easy Recipes from The New York Times

With Jean-Georges Vongerichten

Simple to Spectacular

Jean-Georges: Cooking at Home with a Four-Star Chef

Mark Bittman's Kitchen Express

404 Inspired Seasonal Dishes You Can Make in 20 Minutes or Less

Mark Bittman

Simon & Schuster Paperbacks

New York   London   Toronto   Sydney   New Delhi

Simon & Schuster Paperbacks
A Division of Simon & Schuster, Inc.
1230 Avenue of the Americas
New York, NY 10020

This Simon & Schuster trade paperback edition March 2014

SIMON & SCHUSTER PAPERBACKS and colophon are registered trademarks
of Simon & Schuster, Inc.

For information about special discounts for bulk purchases,
please contact Simon & Schuster Special Sales at
1-866-506-1949 or business@simonandschuster.com.

The Simon & Schuster Speakers Bureau can bring authors to your live event. For more
information or to book an event, contact the Simon & Schuster Speakers Bureau at
1-866-248-3049 or visit our website at www.simonspeakers.com.

Designed by Linda Dingler

Manufactured in the United States of America

2   4   6   8   10   9   7   5   3   1

The Library of Congress has cataloged the hardcover edition as follows:

Bittman, Mark.
Mark Bittman's Kitchen Express : 404 inspired seasonal dishes you can make in 20 minutes or less / Mark Bittman.
p. cm
1. Quick and easy cookery. 2. Cookery, International. I. Title.
TX833.5.B548   2009
641.5'55—dc22   2008054823

ISBN 978-1-4165-7566-5
ISBN 978-1-4767-5765-0 (pbk)
ISBN 978-1-4165-7898-7 (ebook)

CONTENTS

INTRODUCTION
3

HOW TO USE THIS BOOK
5

A WORD ABOUT INGREDIENTS
7

THE *KITCHEN EXPRESS* PANTRY
9

MORE WAYS TO NAVIGATE *KITCHEN EXPRESS*
17

SUMMER
27

FALL
67

WINTER
113

SPRING
157

KITCHEN EXPRESS MENUS
203

OVEN TEMPERATURE EQUIVALENCIES
210

ACKNOWLEDGMENTS
211

INDEX
213

INTRODUCTION

The simple format of *Kitchen Express* belies all that it has to offer. Here are 101 incredibly fast and easy recipes for each season—404 in all. The experienced home cook can play with each to great advantage, yet at their core, they're recipes presented in the simplest form possible, understandable and readily executed by anyone who's done some cooking.

As a group, they are precisely imprecise. This is unusual for recipes, but it's long been my belief that the most specific recipes are the most limiting. Specificity is fine for baking, where the chemistry among the ingredients often determines success or failure. But in savory cooking, where amounts can vary wildly—there's almost never a critical difference between one onion and two: A "head" of broccoli might weigh one or one-and-a-half pounds; a steak may be three-quarters to an inch and a half thick—to try to force cooks to follow recipes demanding precision robs them of the ability to improvise, to relax, to substitute, to use their own judgment.

Jacques Pepin once remarked to me that the old adage about never stepping foot in the same river twice holds true for recipes also: You don't start with the same amount of ingredients, they're not at the same temperature, they're not the same age or from the same place, the ambient temperature and humidity are probably different, as are your equipment and mood. Everything is different, and the results will be too.

These little recipes acknowledge that up front. I don't really care how much garlic you use in most recipes, so "some" is as good as "a teaspoon." Similarly, garnishes are garnishes: You use more, you use less, you leave them out—it shouldn't matter. "A carrot" in a soup could certainly be a big one or a small one, and so on. So I rarely give *exact* measurements, unless proportions are critical.

This style of cooking is about three things: speed, flexibility, and relaxation. If you read one of these recipes, if it inspires you, and if you have the ingredients (or something approximating them) to throw it together—then go into the kitchen, assemble what you need, and have at it. Twenty minutes later, max, you'll be eating something delicious. What's wrong with that?

HOW TO USE THIS BOOK

There are some givens here, and it's worth taking a moment to understand them. I've organized *Kitchen Express* by seasons, not because I think grilling in winter or braising in summer is "inappropriate," but because I wanted to feature the right ingredients at the right time. To me, the organization is not dogmatic, but it is realistic, and it jibes with the current trend among savvy eaters to avoid, for example, Southern Hemisphere fruit in winter. As it happens, asparagus is best in spring, broccoli in fall and spring, corn in summer, and so on. You can cook what you want when you want it, of course, but I think that as you're browsing in *Kitchen Express,* you're best off starting with the season in which you find yourself; chances are you'll find something appealing right there, one that not only uses the best ingredients available but suits your mood. (When all is said and done, grilling in winter works only occasionally for those of us who have real winters, and braising in summer usually requires a pretty hefty dose of air-conditioning.)

How fast are the recipes? In general the speed with which you execute them depends not on how fast you chop (almost everyone chops better and faster than I do, and I can do any of these in 20 minutes or so) but on how well you're organized, and how well you multitask.

If you're the kind of person who organizes everything ahead of time, then spends a while chopping and assembling the ingredients, then hovers over the stove and watches everything develop, stirring and turning carefully and lovingly, that's great, but you should figure that these dishes will take you a little longer. These recipes were developed for the type of cook who gets the oil hot while chopping an onion, cooks the onion while peeling and chopping the carrot, adds the carrot and goes on to dice the meat, and so on—a kind of fast, steady, sequential cooking that is more grandmotherly and short-order than it is haute cuisine.

In fact, this is definitely *not* haute cuisine. It's very good food, done quickly. The idea here is to provide quick, satisfying dishes—delicious dishes. Many are complete meals, but I've often suggested appropriate accompaniments and serving suggestions to fill them out when necessary. These, of course, are optional. Most often they feature quick-cooked or pre-bought ingredients: bread, steamed broccoli, couscous. This doesn't mean that if you have time you can't make brown rice, or your own bread, or a more complicated vegetable dish.

And if you have even less time, open a jar of high-quality pickles; steam a plate of vegetables in the microwave; broil some eggplant slices; shred some cabbage or lettuce and serve the meat or seafood on that (it will wilt and collect the flavorful juices); quickly stir-fry a single vegetable in the same pan you used to cook the main course; have sliced fruit on the side; use a fast-frozen vegetable like peas, rutabaga, or corn; make a quick raw-vegetable salad by grating or chopping whatever you'd like and dressing it in a little oil and vinegar. You get the idea.

By the same token, cooking methods are flexible, especially when it comes to grilling, broiling, or using a grill pan. Do what your equipment and the weather allow. In terms of equipment, I only assume that your kitchen is stocked with a food processor and *probably* a blender.

Generally, the quantities in the recipes here are designed for three or four people. But again, the specifications are loose enough so that it won't take much to tweak them for fewer or more servings to make a meal more substantial, or plan ahead for leftovers. You can also combine the dishes in this book to make a larger dinner or pull together a buffet; check out some suggestions on page 203.

How and when you use the dishes in *Kitchen Express* is equally flexible. Some foods become trans-seasonal simply by swapping out a key ingredient (see "Some Simple Substitutions" on page 15). Others transcend the seasons or may have multiple—or more specific—uses worth highlighting. For help finding recipes using a tool besides the seasonal chapters or the index, see "More Ways to Navigate *Kitchen Express*," beginning on page 17.

A WORD ABOUT INGREDIENTS

The simpler the cooking, the more important the ingredients. The dishes in *Kitchen Express* sometimes feature sophisticated combinations, and the occasional odd ingredient, but at their core they are extremely simple, and they rely on good ingredients (which you're more likely to find in season).

Even when, for the sake of speed, I call for convenience foods like canned beans, stock, or tomatoes, if you can use homemade or fresher versions, the dishes will be all the better. In any case, all your ingredients should be as high quality as you can find. If fresh tomatoes are real and tasty, use 'em, but whenever they're not, canned tomatoes are a better option. And whenever you have time to make stock or beans, for example, from scratch, you should—refrigerate or freeze them for future use and your *Kitchen Express*–style dishes will shine more brightly.

Like many modern cooks, I use extra-virgin olive oil for my cooking fat all the time, unless I want a more neutral flavor (in which case I use grapeseed or another oil), or a different flavor (like peanut), or a higher smoke point (in which case most oils are better than olive). In theory at least, all extra-virgin olive oil is high quality; for other oils, look for those that are cold-pressed or minimally processed.

I use a lot of really fast-cooking ingredients here: boneless meats, plenty of seafood, quick-cooking vegetables, grains like couscous (which is actually not a grain but a pasta) and bulgur (which steeps faster than rice cooks). As a result, as often as not, your rinsing, trimming, peeling, and chopping will take as long as your cooking. (As most veteran cooks know, shopping is the most time-consuming aspect of cooking, so if you keep a well-stocked pantry, you're miles ahead of the game.)

I'm assuming everything you start with is thawed, your shrimp is peeled, your mussels are scrubbed, your poultry is boned, and so on. The cooking methods I use are the quickest: sautéing (which I often call simply "cooking"), boiling, steaming, and grilling (or broiling; anything that can be grilled can be broiled, and vice versa). And I rely heavily on those convenience foods we don't think of as such: prosciutto and bacon, Parmesan and soy—these are ingredients that are front-loaded with time and labor so that we can use them to flavor dishes quickly.

Finally, I have tried my best to make these recipes as uncomplicated as possible, and—counter to my inclinations, and to most of the work I've done in other books—have avoided spelling out as many variations and substitutions as possible. Every cook with even a minimum of experience will quickly realize that string beans can be swapped for asparagus when the latter is unavailable, or that ground turkey (or even ground salmon, or shrimp) can almost always be substituted for ground beef. (See the table on page 15 for some more examples of easy substitutions.) You can't make a roast chicken without a chicken, it's true, but very few of the ingredients in these (or other) recipes are sacred. The goals are these: Get good food onto the table, fast, and have fun doing so.

THE *KITCHEN EXPRESS* PANTRY

Over the years, I've cooked substantial meals in the tiniest, most poorly equipped kitchens—even non-kitchens—that you can imagine. So I can say with the utmost confidence that the size of your larder is less important than how you stock it. It's equally true that the more you cook—and the more varied your recipe repertoire—the deeper your pantry will be, as you collect a range of global ingredients that reflect the way you like to eat.

Since this book assumes you're an enthusiastic cook, it also assumes you already have a well-stocked pantry. What follows, then, are specific lists of the foods you should keep handy if you want to cook in the style I'm outlining here.

Must your pantry contain these exact staples? Of course not. You will naturally gravitate toward the flavors and ingredients you prefer, and I've noted the cases that reflect some of these potential preferences. But cooking at home becomes exponentially easier, faster, and more spontaneous when you have basic foods at arm's reach.

In the Cupboard

These are all shelf-stable products that should be stored at room temperature (cool room temperature is best, though obviously not always possible), preferably in the dark (or at least out of direct sunlight). This list starts with the ones you're likely to use most, and I've noted the semi-perishable foods to consider freezing or refrigerating if you don't go through them fast. In general, replace anything else on this list every year or so.

Oils: Extra-virgin olive oil, and at least one vegetable oil (I like grapeseed or peanut oil) for when you want something neutral for Asian cooking or at other times when olive oil is too strong. Sesame oil is nice for drizzling, and a little goes a long way. Choose high-quality, minimally processed oils for the purest flavors; and if you don't go through them very fast, store the bottles in the fridge.

Vinegars: Sherry vinegar (which is higher in acidity than other types) is my favorite, though a good white wine vinegar is also useful. Balsamic and rice vinegars have no replacements, and with their relatively low acidity they work more like condiments than stronger vinegars.

Sauces: Soy, hot pepper, nam pla (Thai fish sauce), hoisin sauce, and maybe Worcestershire sauce are the only ones you need. If you don't make your own salsa or barbecue sauce, then maybe you want good-quality store-bought bottles of these on hand, too.

Condiments: Mustard (maybe more than one kind), ketchup, and mayonnaise (again, if you don't make your own). Though I'm not a fan of vinegary pickles and relishes, a lot of people are. And capers are endlessly useful. Once all these condiments are open, store them in the fridge if you're worried about leaving them at room temperature for long.

Canned Tomatoes and Paste: Whole plum tomatoes are better than diced. Just break them up with your hands right in the can and pull out the tough core; or take them out and roughly chop as you would a fresh tomato. If you don't need the juice, refrigerate it to drink or use later. The handiest way to buy tomato paste is in tubes, but if you can't find it that way, small cans or jars are fine. When I say "a can of tomatoes" I mean the standard-size can (which runs about 15 ounces), unless a large (28-ounce) can or other quantity is specified.

Stock: This is a tough one because premade stock is not a tenth as good as even the fastest batch you can whip up yourself; but it's undeniably convenient. So if you find a brand you can tolerate, keep it on hand. Water is a good substitute in most cases, and I rely on it more and more.

Rice: White long-grain rice can be ready in 20 minutes; short-grain is a little faster. Brown rice takes about twice as long. But the good news about all of these (as well as the grains that follow) is that once cooked, they keep in the fridge for several days and reheat well in the microwave. So cooking in bulk ahead of time is an option, too.

Quick-Cooking Grains: White or whole wheat couscous (which is actually a pasta) and bulgur require only steeping. If you're willing to wait 20 to 30 minutes for grains to get tender, you might want to try steel-cut oats, cracked wheat, kasha, or quinoa.

Pasta: Like rice, pasta can be ready by the time the main recipe is. Include enough time to bring a pot of water to a boil (putting a lid on it really helps speed things up). Keep long strands or cut noodles handy—whatever you like. The thinner the pasta, though, the quicker the cooking time, so if you're really pressed, think angel hair.

Asian Noodles: Rice sticks, rice vermicelli, and bean threads (sometimes called glass noodles) all get tender after 10 minutes or so of soaking in hot water. Soba, somen, udon, and dried Chinese egg noodles require cooking but generally take less time than Italian pasta; the fresh kinds take only a minute or two.

Beans: Chickpeas, cannellini, pinto, and black beans. Canned beans are one solution, since you obviously can't cook dried beans in less than 20 minutes (though lentils and split peas almost make the cut). But if you cook a pot of lightly seasoned dried beans, then freeze them in small portions along with some of the cooking liquid, you can essentially stock your own "canned" beans. Only these will be infinitely better. (When I say "a can of beans" I mean the standard can, about 15 ounces, which equals about two cups.)

Crackers, Croutons, and Breadcrumbs: Preferably homemade. Tightly sealed, they'll keep longer than you think. Panko breadcrumbs are my favorite store-bought variety because they're big and crunchy.

Flours: For the cooking in this book, you generally won't need more than small quantities of white flour—usually for dredging—or sometimes cornmeal. If you don't bake regularly, refrigerate or freeze flours in tightly sealed containers or bags.

Dried Fruit, Including Dried Tomatoes: They keep so well, don't take up much room, and quickly add heft, flavor, and nutrition to many pasta, meat, and poultry dishes.

Chocolate, Nuts, and Seeds: Not just for snacking, but for cooking too. Almonds, hazelnuts, and peanuts are basic, as are sesame, pumpkin, or sunflower seeds; shredded unsweetened coconut is also useful. Keep them in the freezer if you don't use them within a month. For chocolate I generally stick to bittersweet with a high percentage of cacao. Unsweetened cocoa powder is nice to have around, and it keeps forever, too.

Onions, Shallots, Garlic, and Ginger: The so-called aromatic vegetables. Keep them at room temperature as long as possible, then move them to the fridge if they start to shrivel. If you want to keep a knob of ginger for a long time, wrap it well and freeze it, or trim off any rough spots and drop it into a small jar of vodka, close the lid, and store it in the fridge.

Potatoes and Sweet Potatoes: You won't have time to bake or roast them with the recipes here, but they cook fast if you cut them small or grate them.

Canned Fish: Oil-packed chunk light tuna is what I recommend for the dishes in this book. It also wouldn't hurt to keep a can each of whole sardines and anchovies and good-quality Alaskan salmon on hand.

Canned Vegetables: None—with the sole exceptions of chiles, like chipotle in adobo sauce, roasted green chiles, or roasted red peppers.

Salt and Pepper: Kosher salt rather than iodized table salt. (Good sea salt, like fleur de sel, is also handy; use it as a condiment.) Whole peppercorns to grind as you use them are a must. If you haven't done so already, invest in a good grinder; you'll notice the difference immediately.

Spices: You can't have too many, but start with cumin, mustard, saffron, cinnamon, coriander, dried chiles, and blends like curry and chili powders. I try to toast and grind my own, but it's not always practical; buy ground when necessary.

Herbs: Few dried herbs are worth the price, but oregano, thyme, rosemary, dill, and tarragon can be useful. I shop at Penzey's (www.penzeys.com) for dried herbs and spices.

On the Counter

A Big Bowl of Fresh Stuff: Seasonal fruit, including tomatoes. Vegetables that don't require refrigeration, like chiles, avocados, and squashes.

Bread: A crusty loaf, a package of pita, or whole wheat or rye sandwich bread.

In the Fridge

Bacon and/or Pancetta: Buy the good stuff in small quantities, either thick-cut or in chunks or slabs. These cured meats keep for a couple of weeks in the fridge; months if you wrap them well and freeze them.

Smoked Ham and/or Prosciutto: Ditto here; when you want thin slices (which you will), just slice your own from larger pieces.

Fresh Meat, Fish, or Poultry: If you shop every few days (or more often) chances are you have something in the fridge for dinner tonight. See the section on substitutions (page 15) for ideas about how to work what you've got into the dishes described in the book.

These days, cooking with seafood warrants a special mention. If you want to choose species that are fished or farmed sustainably—and you should—or if you're worried about mercury or other contaminants, then you have to do a little research, and not just once but on an ongoing basis. I suggest using the Monterey Bay Aquarium's "Seafood Watch" (www.montereybayquarium.org). The list and its rankings change frequently, and though I don't consider it perfect, this organization provides the most reliable and accessible tool for helping you make informed decisions.

The recipes here are designed to be flexible, so I usually call simply for "fish" and provide some guidance if necessary in the headnote. The exceptions are when I call for salmon (use wild if at all possible), scallops, tuna (not bluefin), sardines and anchovies, clams or mussels, crab, squid, lobster, and shrimp (again, wild), for which tasty, safe, and sustainable options are readily available, and substitutions are a little trickier.

Leftover Cooked Meat, Fish, or Poultry: These increase your options, as do cooked deli meats like roast beef, corned beef, rotisserie chicken, and turkey. All of these have a life beyond sandwiches, as some of these recipes suggest.

Eggs: Essential.

Cheese and Dairy: Parmesan—the real stuff, from Italy—is a must, and keeps for months as long as you buy it in chunks, not pre-grated. Other cheeses: sharp cheddar, Gruyère or another nutty melting cheese, and something fresh like mozzarella, feta, goat cheese, or queso fresco. For cooking, half-and-half or heavy cream is more useful than milk, but if you drink milk you already have it around, so that's fine. Butter: unsalted, please. And sour cream and/or yogurt: At least occasionally, I prefer the full-fat kinds.

Long-Keeping Vegetables: Carrots, celery, broccoli, cauliflower, cabbage, Brussels sprouts, eggplant, string beans, and summer squashes all keep for at least a week and are available virtually all year long. I also try to keep some fresh greens in the house for salads or stir-fries.

Long-Keeping Fruit: Lemons, always. Limes are nice for a change and virtually interchangeable with lemons. Oranges and grapefruit in the winter; apples and pineapples when they're good.

Olives: Pick your favorite kinds; they're virtually interchangeable.

Miso: Keeps forever and can produce a complex-tasting stock, sauce, dressing, or marinade in minutes. White is the mildest, red is the strongest, and brown (made with rice or barley) falls somewhere in between.

Fresh Herbs: Tricky. They can be expensive, and they have a short shelf life, but they're invaluable in quick-cooking dishes. So I suggest you always have a bunch of parsley in the fridge. Beyond that, pick, say, one or two fresh herbs—oregano, sage, basil, chives, rosemary, cilantro, whatever—to buy each week. All fresh herbs store best like flowers in a little jar of water. Cover the tops loosely with a plastic bag and pluck leaves or stems as you need them.

In the Freezer

Meat and Poultry: Ground meat, chops, steaks, cutlets, and chicken parts all do well in the freezer provided they're well wrapped to prevent freezer burn. (The only problem is that you've got to plan in advance before using them.) It's safest to thaw animal foods in the refrigerator, but this process can take a couple of days. Your second choice is to soak the food in cold water. (The microwave does not thaw properly.) Fish doesn't keep well in most home freezers.

Frozen Vegetables: No apologies. I'm a fan of frozen peas, edamame, and other fresh beans (like lima, fava, or black-eyed peas). Frozen corn kernels, spinach, and hearty greens like mustard or collards, rutabagas, and bell peppers are good, too. I don't bother with carrots or string beans, or anything sauced or seasoned.

Frozen Fruits: These are fine for cooking and smoothies. Frozen raspberries, blackberries, and blueberries are better than frozen strawberries.

A Loaf of Really Good Bread: I keep a couple of baguettes in the freezer all the time. It's not always possible to monitor the progress of the bread on the counter, and you don't want to be stuck without any.

Anything You Make Yourself: Tomato sauce, beans, and stock especially. I can't stress this enough.

Some Simple Substitutions

You can change virtually any recipe in the book according to season and work around whatever ingredients you have on hand (and remember that you can read this list back and forth from left to right or right to left).

FOODS	EASY SUBSTITUTIONS
Lettuce and salad greens like arugula, mesclun, iceberg, romaine, spinach, and so on	Raw, they're all virtually interchangeable.
Tender greens for cooking, like spinach or arugula	Watercress, thinly sliced napa cabbage
Heartier greens for cooking, like kale, chard, mustard, or bok choy	All interchangeable; cooking time will vary depending on thickness.
Shallots	Any onion, especially red
Parsnips	Carrots
Fennel	Celery
Cauliflower	Broccoli
Asparagus	String beans
Brussels sprouts	Cabbage
Fava beans	Lima beans or edamame (frozen are fine)
Jicama	Radishes, especially daikon
Eggplant	Zucchini
Apples	Pears
Mango	Papaya
Strawberries	Pineapple
Basil	Cilantro, mint, chives, or even parsley
Shrimp	Scallops, squid, or crawfish; or cut-up chicken or pork
Lump crabmeat	Cooked lobster or shrimp
Boneless chicken breasts	Boneless chicken thighs (they generally take a little longer to cook); pork, turkey, or veal cutlets
Chicken (cutlets, boneless parts, or cut up for stir-fry)	Pork (chops, tenderloin medallions, or cut-up shoulder), or turkey
Ground beef	Ground pork, turkey, chicken, or lamb
Beef steaks	Pork or lamb chops
Nam pla (Thai fish sauce)	Soy sauce
Sour cream	Yogurt

MORE WAYS TO NAVIGATE
KITCHEN EXPRESS

Dishes That Double as Appetizers

These make fabulous first courses in a more formal meal (you can also start with salad or soup, of course; see pages 227 and 230 of the Index). For finger food, see the list on page 20.

Wild Mushroom Crostini (page 128)
Snap Peas with Walnuts and Roquefort (page 175)
Seared Fish with Lettuce Leaves (page 176)
Garlic-Ginger Shrimp (page 180)
Mark's Famous Spicy Shrimp (page 180)
Carne Cruda (page 190)
Herbed Fresh Cheese Patties (page 198)
Sausage and Grape Bruschetta (page 40)
Black and Blue Tuna (page 47)
Grilled Watermelon and Shrimp Skewers (page 50)
Crab Cake Burger (page 51)
Egg and Carrot Cake with Soy (page 70)
White Bean Toasts (page 79)
Figs in a Blanket (page 80)
West Indian Pork Kebabs (page 99)

Brown-Bag Lunches

Leftover pasta, soup, and main courses; salads and cold sandwiches—these are all no-brainers for workplace lunches. So here are some of the less obvious one-dish meals that travel well from fridge to desk or corporate kitchen; some of them benefit from reheating. Some can be eaten as is, at work or (if you're lucky) on a bench, or at a park or beach.

Quick Cassoulet (page 122)
Tofu with Pineapple and Red Peppers (page 130)
Seafood Couscous (page 134)
Fish with Edamame Pesto (page 178)
Herbed Fresh Cheese Patties (page 198)
Chicken with Chinese Long Beans and Lemongrass (page 54)
Grilled Chicken Paillards with Endive and Radicchio (page 53)
Hot-and-Sour Beef and Okra Stir-fry (page 59)
Egg and Carrot Cake with Soy (page 70)
Flatbread Pizza with Figs, Goat Cheese, and Balsamic (page 83)
Butter Beans with Prosciutto and Mushrooms (page 84)
Eggplant Rolls (page 87)

Breakfasts and Brunches You Can Eat Any Time of the Year

Change the fruit, vegetables, or seasonings and these eye-openers are fine in any season.

Eggs 'n' Capers (page 116)
Pancetta and Spinach Frittata (page 115)
Japanese Egg Crepes (page 116)
Bacon, Eggs, and Grits (page 116)
Eggs in a Hole with 'Shrooms (page 115)
Leek, Sun-Dried Tomato, and Goat Cheese Frittata (page 117)
Fried Eggs with Lemon and Chervil (page 159)
Mixed Herb Omelet (page 160)
Chilaquiles (page 159)

Hangtown Fry (page 160)

Blueberry Pancakes (page 29)

Muesli with Raspberries (page 29)

Matzo Brei with Cherries (page 30)

Tomato, Goat Cheese, and Basil Strata (page 30)

Mediterranean Poached Eggs (page 69)

Spicy Escarole with Croutons and Eggs (page 69)

Huevos Rancheros (page 70)

Breakfast Burritos (page 70)

Brunch Baked Eggs (page 71)

Migas (page 33)

Desserts You Can Eat Any Time of the Year

Some desserts are bound to their season, but you can enjoy many others year-round. Then there are those that change character, and season, when you change the fruit.

Lemon Mascarpone Mousse (page 153)

Grapefruit 'n' Cream Shake (page 153)

Orange Fool (page 154)

Almond Tart (page 155)

Nutella Fondue (page 155)

Deconstructed Raspberry Soufflés (page 198)

Rose Water Whipped Cream with Honeydew (page 198)

Grilled Angel Food Cake with Fruit Salsa (page 199)

Ginger-Lemon "Ice Cream" (page 64)

Peach Lemon "Cheesecake" (page 65)

Fresh Fruit Gratin (page 65)

Blueberry Ricotta Cheesecakes (page 63)

Apricot Cream Upside-Down Pie (page 64)

Ice Cream Sandwich (page 66)

Caramelized Pears with Mascarpone (page 109)

Finger Food for All Occasions

Perfect for cocktail parties or picnics. Serve these with toothpicks alongside, or cut them into bite-size triangles, squares, or chunks, before or after preparing. For a list of more substantial knife-and-fork appetizers, see page 17.

Fondue (page 129)
Simplest Chicken Kebabs (page 136)
Scallion-Stuffed Beef Rolls (page 145)
Indian-Style Lamb Kebabs (page 147)
Chickpea Burgers (made bite-size) (page 173)
Cheese "Burger" (made bite-size) (page 172)
Middle Eastern Pizza (page 173)
Chicken Satay with Peanut Sauce (page 187)
Chicken with Coconut and Lime (page 187)
Deviled Eggs with Crab (page 30)
Duck Wraps with Plums (page 39)
Summer Rolls with Barbecued Pork (page 39)
Grilled Fish Kebabs (page 48)
Shrimp, Scallop, and Cherry Tomato Kebabs (page 51)
Grilled Pork Skewers with Worcestershire (page 56)
Sesame Shrimp Toasts (page 92)

Recipes That Barely Disturb the Kitchen

No recipe in this book leaves you with a sink full of dirty dishes, but here are those which really can be made in one pan or pot, with a minimum of mess.

Japanese Egg Crepes (page 116)
Fondue (page 129)
Potato Cumin Curry (page 132)
Broiled Squid (page 134)
Lemon Mascarpone Mousse (page 153)
Miso Soup with Tofu (page 162)

Udon Noodles with Green Tea Broth (page 161)

Tuna and Bean Salad (page 170)

Fast Fish Soup (page 164)

Classic Caesar Salad (page 165)

Tuna with Pineapple, Cucumber, and Avocado (page 48)

Ice Cream Sandwich (page 66)

Pound Cake with Mascarpone and Marmalade (page 110)

Brown Sugar Apple in the Microwave (page 111)

The Easiest of the Easiest

Of all the recipes in *Kitchen Express,* these are the ones that give the biggest rewards for the smallest amount of work.

Zuppa di Pane (page 119)

Avocado, Citrus, and Radicchio Salad (page 125)

Mussels in White Wine and Garlic (page 133)

Citrus-Braised Fish Fillets or Steaks (page 135)

Chicken Piccata (page 141)

Sausage and Potatoes (page 142)

Linguine with Butter, Parmesan, and Sage (page 149)

Warm Milk Toast (page 152)

Chive Salad (page 167)

Lemon Parmesan Chicken (page 186)

Avocado Soup with Crab (page 32)

Sesame Shrimp Toasts (page 92)

Mussels in Tomato–White Bean Sauce (page 92)

Nutella Fondue (page 155)

The Best Recipes for Picnics

Any sandwich—and there are dozens of them here—is fine for a picnic. But here are some additional, perhaps unexpected, ideas.

Raw Beet Salad (page 124)
Cajun-Style Salmon (page 178)
Chicken Tandoori (page 183)
Rice Noodles with Cilantro Pesto (page 196)
Panzanella (page 34)
Tuna Tabouleh (page 34)
Black Bean and Mango Salad (page 34)
Four-Bean Salad (page 36)
Microwaved Honey Eggplant (page 44)
Grilled Lemon-Tarragon Chicken (page 52)
Greek-Style Eggplant Salad (page 77)
Seared Cauliflower with Olives and Breadcrumbs (page 82)
Chicken with Sweet-and-Sour Sherry Sauce (page 94)
Pound Cake with Mascarpone and Marmalade (page 110)

The Best Recipes for Reheating

Any soup can be reheated; here are some other dishes that you can warm on the stove, in the oven, or in the microwave.

Mixed Bean Soup or Stew (page 120)
Lima Bean Stew (page 121)
Quick Cassoulet (page 122)
Mixed Bean Chili (page 122)
Braised Cabbage with Spanish Chorizo and Beans (page 130)
Chicken Poached in Port (page 141)
Crisp Fennel Gratin (page 175)
Butter Beans with Prosciutto and Mushrooms (page 84)
Braised Chicken with Olives and Raisins (page 93)

Lavender-Thyme Braised Chicken (page 94)
Chicken Curry in a Hurry (page 95)
Braised Pork with Rosemary (page 97)
Fennel-Orange Braised Pork (page 97)
Sausage with Red Lentils (page 99)
Sausage and Cabbage (page 98)
Braised Lamb Chops with Prunes (page 103)
Pasta Gratinée (page 108)

The Best Do-Ahead Recipes for Potlucks

Need to carry a dish to someone else's house? Try one of these.

Banderilla Pasta (page 148)
Pasta with Tomato Tapenade (page 149)
Lebanese Potato Salad (page 169)
Crisp Fennel Gratin (page 175)
Pasta with Moroccan Tapenade (page 194)
Warm Corn Salad with Ham (page 37)
Taco Slaw (page 44)
Swiss Chard with White Beans and Pancetta (page 45)
Poached Tofu with Broccoli (page 63)
Pasta Salad with Beans and Herbs (page 61)
Pasta with Cherry Tomatoes (page 61)
Almond Tart (page 155)
Broiled Brussels Sprouts with Hazelnuts (page 82)
Root Vegetable Stir-Fry (page 83)

Recipes for Hot Sandwiches

Terrific dishes for serving between two pieces of bread, stuffed into a split roll or pocket pita, wrapped up in a large warm tortilla, or open-face on thick slices of toast.

Sweet Sauerkraut with Kielbasa (page 142)

Hangtown Fry (page 160)

Eggs Bhona (page 160)

Jerk Chicken (page 54)

Spiced Chicken with Mango Salsa (page 55)

Spicy Grilled Pork with Peach Marmalade (page 56)

Korean Barbecued Beef (page 58)

Grilled Skirt Steak with Tomatillo Salsa (page 58)

Northern Beans with Spanish Chorizo (page 87)

Ham Steak with Redeye Gravy (page 100)

Recipes to Toss with Pasta

All of these are moist enough to serve as a sauce when mixed with a pound or more of cooked pasta.

Fish Braised in Lemon with Tomatoes and Red Peppers (page 177)

Chicken with Bacon, Shallots, and Brandy (page 140)

Mark's Famous Spicy Shrimp (page 180)

Mediterranean Chicken (page 183)

Chicken with Green Olives (page 185)

Zucchini with Tomatoes and Chorizo (page 46)

Garlicky Rabe with Pancetta and Pine Nuts (page 85)

Fried Endive with Butter and Lemon Sauce (page 86)

Seared Tuna with Capers and Tomatoes (page 90)

Braised Fish with Zucchini (page 88)

Chicken Puttanesca (page 96)

Recipes to Serve over Asian Noodles or Rice

Not every stir-fry dish mandates rice or noodles, but on the other hand, why not? The meal expands almost instantly.

Crisp Tofu and Asian Greens with Peanut Sauce (page 131)

Shrimp with Black Bean Sauce (page 133)

Chicken in Spicy Basil-Coconut Sauce (page 136)

Ketchup-Braised Tofu with Veggies (page 174)

Garlic-Ginger Shrimp (page 180)

Spicy Chicken with Lemongrass and Lime (page 184)

Broiled Eggplant with Miso-Walnut Vinaigrette (page 39)

Stir-Fried Corn and Clams (page 52)

Chicken with Chinese Long Beans and Lemongrass (page 54)

Hot-and-Sour Beef and Okra Stir-fry (page 59)

Stir-fried Mixed Vegetables with Ginger (page 85)

Eggplant Stir-fry (page 86)

Crisp Tofu 'n' Bok Choy (page 87)

Stir-fried Shrimp with Chestnuts and Napa Cabbage (page 90)

Stir-fried Chicken with Nuts (page 93)

Chicken Teriyaki Skewers (page 96)

Soups You Can Chill

Perfect hot-weather soups.

Peanut Soup (page 117)

Cauliflower Soup (page 117)

Asparagus Leek Soup (page 163)

Zucchini and Dill Soup (page 31)

Curried Coconut–Butternut Squash Soup (page 73)

Summer

The explosion of universally

available fruits and vegetables makes cooking naturally quicker and more varied in summer than it is in other seasons, with the possible exception of fall. And the fact that this produce includes items almost everyone loves—tomatoes, corn, stone fruit, and much more—makes pleasing people easy. Almost as interesting to the cook is the abundance of herbs: These allow you to vary your favorite dishes by doing little more than switching a tablespoon of this for a tablespoon of that.

1.

Blueberry Pancakes

Substitute cornmeal for up to half of the flour, for crunch.

Combine two cups flour, two teaspoons baking powder, one-quarter teaspoon salt, and one tablespoon of sugar. Whisk two eggs with one and one-half cups milk and two tablespoons melted butter. Add wet ingredients to dry; stir to combine (it's OK if there are some lumps). Cook with butter—make them big or small, your call—scattering blueberries on top of each cake; flip after the batter begins to bubble. Serve however you like.

2.

Muesli with Raspberries

In the winter, try this with dried cherries.

In a large bowl combine rolled oats (*not* the quick-cooking kind) with a mixture of chopped nuts and seeds; the usual ratio is three parts oats to two parts extras, but do whatever you like. Toss in some shredded coconut, a little brown sugar and cinnamon, and a pinch of salt. Serve with yogurt and fresh raspberries, drizzled with honey. Store the leftovers as you would granola.

3.

Matzo Brei with Cherries

To go savory, skip the maple syrup and add some fresh chopped sage or rosemary and lots of black pepper.

Pit a couple of cups of tart cherries (or use frozen; don't bother to thaw them). For every egg (or two if you want more egg than cracker), run a sheet of matzo under cold water until it's barely soft. Fry the damp crackers in lots of butter over medium-high heat, tossing and breaking them up a bit. When they start to crisp up, add the cherries and cook until dry. Then stir in the scrambled eggs with a pinch of salt and cook them until just set. Serve drizzled with maple syrup.

4.

Deviled Eggs with Crab

Buy fresh crabmeat if you can or use chopped cooked shrimp.

Make hard-cooked eggs; meanwhile, combine crabmeat with a spoonful each of Dijon mustard and mayonnaise or yogurt, lemon juice, diced red bell pepper, paprika, and cumin; sprinkle with salt and pepper. Run eggs under cold water, shell and halve them, and mash the yolks into the crab mixture; stuff the whites. Sprinkle the top with chopped parsley (or caviar for that matter).

5.

Tomato, Goat Cheese, and Basil Strata

You can assemble this the night before and refrigerate until you're ready to bake.

Heat the oven to 400°F. Soften a chopped onion in butter; off heat, stir in chopped fresh tomato, six beaten eggs, a cup fresh shredded basil, a splash of milk or cream, and a sprinkle of salt and pepper. Top with bread cubes and dollops of goat cheese. Bake until just set, about 20 minutes; put under broiler quickly to brown top if necessary.

6.

Gazpacho

Try peaches or melons instead of tomatoes, or add anchovies for more flavor.

Core and seed ripe, juicy tomatoes and cut into chunks. Peel and seed a cucumber and roughly chop. Peel a clove or two of garlic. Cut the crusts from a couple of thick slices of good white bread and tear them up. Puree everything in a blender with salt, pepper, lots of olive oil, and a splash of sherry vinegar, adding just enough water (or ice) to thin the mixture. Serve garnished with a drizzle of olive oil and chopped basil or mint leaves.

7.

Zucchini and Dill Soup

Add fresh ricotta, sour cream, or yogurt while pureeing, for richness.

Grate a couple of zucchini. Cook a chopped onion in butter until softened, then add the zucchini and stir until softened, five minutes or so. Add vegetable or chicken stock and bring to a boil; simmer for about five minutes, then puree until smooth. Season with salt and pepper and lots of fresh chopped dill.

8.

Shrimp and Tomato Soup

Amazing with good tomatoes.

Boil one pound of shell-on shrimp in six cups of water until just pink; drain, reserving the liquid. Cook a chopped shallot in some olive oil (you can use the same pot), sprinkle with salt and pepper, and deglaze with a splash of white wine or dry vermouth. Add the reserved liquid and let bubble a bit; peel and chop the shrimp. Cut two or three ripe tomatoes into wedges and add them to the pot, along with the shrimp and chopped fresh tarragon. When just warmed through, serve in shallow bowls.

9.

Melon Soup with Pancetta

Sweet and salty.

Puree the flesh from a cantaloupe or honeydew with lemon juice and a little white wine or water until smooth. Put the soup in the freezer to chill (along with some serving bowls if you like) while you frizzle some thin ribbons of pancetta or prosciutto in a little olive oil. When crisp, add several grinds of black pepper and remove from heat. To serve, put the soup in bowls, and top with ham, chives, salt, and pan drippings.

10.

Avocado Soup with Crab

Lightning-fast luxury; instead of the crab, try cooked shrimp or lobster.
Or use tortilla chips, ripe tomato chunks, or crumbled queso fresco.

Puree a couple of ripe avocados with two cups of whole milk and a pinch of salt. Season a mound of fresh lump crabmeat with minced fresh red chiles, chopped cilantro, and a squeeze of lime or orange juice. Serve the soup with a scoop of the crab.

11.

Smoke 'n' Spice Fish Soup

Almost any seafood works here, as do bits of cooked chicken.

Chop an onion, a carrot, and a couple of celery stalks and cook in olive oil with minced garlic and salt and pepper until soft. Chop as much canned chipotle as you like (for less heat, remove the seeds) and add it to the soup along with some of its sauce (adobo) and six cups of chicken or fish stock (or water). Boil, then lower the heat a bit and add two or three chopped ripe tomatoes. When the mixture boils again, lay a couple white fish fillets in the soup, turn the heat to low, cover, and cook for about five more minutes. Break the fish into large chunks and serve with a dollop of sour cream, chopped cilantro, and warm tortillas.

12.

Charred Tomato Bisque

Good hot or cold.

Heat the broiler. Cut four or six large ripe tomatoes into thin slices and spread them out on a rimmed baking sheet, along with three smashed garlic cloves, olive oil, salt, and pepper. Broil until the tomatoes are beginning to blacken, turning as necessary, about eight minutes total; remove the garlic as soon as it turns golden. Puree everything with a cup of cream and a half-cup of basil leaves. Warm gently in a saucepan or chill for a few minutes in the freezer. Serve with grilled cheese sandwiches or breadsticks.

13.

Migas

Crouton hash, really; in place of the beans, any kind of protein works,
from eggs (raw or hard-boiled) to nuts to sliced chorizo.

Cut several slices of old bread into cubes. Heat a film of olive oil in a large skillet and fry the bread, seasoning with salt, pepper, pimentón, and cumin as it cooks. Remove to a large bowl, add a little more oil to the pan if necessary, and cook precooked or canned chickpeas until they're golden and beginning to crisp. Cut a bunch of Swiss chard into ribbons and add that to the pan. Stir-fry until the greens wilt, then toss the mixture with the bread cubes. Serve with lemon wedges.

14.

Goat Cheese Salad

Serve on a bed of greens, on slices of toasted bread, or on a baked potato.

Mash soft goat cheese with a tiny bit of minced garlic, salt and pepper, chopped fresh mint, thinly sliced red onion, chopped ripe tomato, and olive oil. Add a handful of pine nuts or pistachios if you like.

15.

Panzanella

Chewy and juicy all in one bite.

Cut ciabatta or other good bread into cubes. Chop ripe tomatoes, oil-cured black olives, anchovies, garlic, and capers; combine with red wine vinegar, olive oil, and lots of black pepper. Add the bread, tossing to absorb the dressing. Garnish with fresh chopped basil and shaved Parmesan cheese.

16.

Tuna Tabouleh

Serve on romaine leaves with tomato and yogurt.

Soak about one-half cup of fine-grain bulgur in boiling water to cover. Peel, seed, and chop a cucumber and toss with lots and lots of chopped parsley, scallions, and fresh mint. Squeeze the bulgur dry and add to the cucumber mixture, dressing with lemon juice (again: lots), olive oil, salt, and pepper. Use a fork to add a can or two of good-quality tuna; toss to fluff the salad and serve.

17.

Black Bean and Mango Salad

Super-colorful, and great wrapped in a flour tortilla with shredded lettuce.

Rinse and drain a can of black beans (or use a couple cups of homemade beans) and combine with a diced mango, a chopped red bell pepper, two or three chopped scallions, and some minced fresh chile. Drizzle with olive oil, lime juice, salt, and pepper. Toss with fresh chopped mint or cilantro and serve.

18.

Mexican Dry-Corn Salad

Use frozen corn if you're feeling lazy.

Heat olive oil in a large skillet over medium-high heat. Add a small chopped red onion, a couple of cups of corn kernels, and a diced fresh chile; cook and stir until the corn is browned. Mash an avocado with a dollop of sour cream or plain yogurt and a squeeze of fresh lime or lemon juice; add chopped cilantro and sprinkle with salt and pepper. Toss the avocado mixture with the corn and serve in a bowl with some shredded iceberg lettuce, chopped tomato, and tortilla chips.

19.

Squid Salad with Basil Mayo

Try stuffing this in tomatoes.

Heat a grill or broiler. Toss whole, cleaned squid with olive oil and salt and pepper. Grill or broil for about two minutes on each side or until opaque but still tender. Meanwhile, toss together sliced radishes, chopped red bell pepper, thinly sliced red onion, and a squeeze of lemon; set aside. Finely chop one cup of fresh basil and stir in one-half cup of mayonnaise. When the squid is cool, cut into rings and toss with the radish mixture; serve on salad greens with a dollop of the mayonnaise on top.

20.

Summertime Shrimp Salad

Toss shelled shrimp in olive oil, salt, and pepper, and grill or broil until cooked through. Zest and juice a lemon and combine with olive oil, chopped cilantro, salt, and pepper. Add diced red onion, chopped cucumber, and chunks of ripe peaches, plums, or melon. Serve the shrimp on top or chop it up a bit and mix it right in the salad.

21.

Soba Noodles and Cucumber with Dipping Sauce

Perfect hot-weather food; add a bit of freshly grated ginger or wasabi for more spice and top with bits of cooked meat or tofu if you like.

Boil and salt water for pasta; meanwhile, combine a quarter cup of chicken stock or water, three tablespoons of soy sauce, two tablespoons of mirin, and a teaspoon of sugar in a bowl; mix to dissolve the sugar. Cook the noodles for about four minutes, then rinse under cold water. Serve a nest of the noodles along with sliced cucumbers in a bowl (set over ice cubes if you like), with a small bowl of the dipping sauce on the side, garnished with chopped scallions.

22.

Four-Bean Salad

A great picnic salad, because the beans only get better as they marinate in the dressing.

Cut about a cup of green beans into one-inch pieces and blanch in boiling, salted water until crisp-tender; drain and run under cold water to stop the cooking. In a bowl, combine a cup or two each of cooked or canned (drain first) kidney or other red beans, cannellini or other white beans, and chickpeas. Add the green beans, a small, diced red onion, and some chopped parsley or chives. Dress with olive oil, sherry vinegar or some other good strong vinegar, Dijon mustard, salt, and pepper.

23.

Prosciutto, Peach, and Mozzarella Salad

Salty, sweet, creamy, and unbeatable.

For each person, cut a fresh peach into eight wedges. Tear prosciutto and sliced mozzarella into bite-size pieces. Dress mixed greens with olive oil, lemon juice, and salt and pepper. Toss in the peaches, prosciutto, and cheese and serve.

24.

Warm Corn Salad with Ham

Like substantial succotash.

Put a half pound or so of good chopped ham into a hot skillet with a little olive oil and a chopped onion. Brown, stirring once in a while. Add the kernels stripped from four ears of corn, along with a handful of frozen lima or fava beans; sprinkle with salt and pepper. Remove from heat and stir in a splash of wine vinegar and some chopped fresh parsley or sage. Serve with thick tomato slices.

25.

Avocado Crab Salad
with Mixed Herb Salad

An impressive, restaurant-style dish.

Whisk together sherry or rice vinegar, Dijon mustard, olive oil, minced shallot, and some salt and pepper. Halve avocados and remove the pits (leave the skin on); cut a thin piece off the bottom of each half so it sits on a plate. Make a salad of fresh herb leaves and sprigs, using chervil, parsley, tarragon, dill, mint, or basil in any combination. Fill each avocado half with lump crabmeat and put a handful of the herbs and a few thin slices of lemon alongside. Drizzle the dressing over all.

26.

Shrimp and Cherry Tomato Salad

Soy sauce is the secret ingredient here.

Stir-fry peeled chopped shrimp and grated ginger in a little sesame oil. Set aside while you halve a pint or two of cherry tomatoes and toss in a salad bowl with a splash of soy sauce. Add the shrimp mixture and a handful of fresh basil (preferably Thai); let rest for a couple of minutes and then serve, with rice crackers.

27.

Arugula with Balsamic Strawberries and Goat Cheese

A surprisingly wonderful salad.

Hull and slice a pint of strawberries and put them in a large salad bowl. Toss with two tablespoons balsamic vinegar and several grinds of black pepper. Let sit for five minutes. Add a bunch of arugula, some crumbled goat cheese, and a sprinkle of salt; drizzle with olive oil, toss, and serve.

28.

Feta and Watermelon Salad

A terrific combination.

Combine watermelon balls (or cubes) in a bowl with crumbled feta cheese, sliced radishes, chopped fresh chives, and a few drops of olive oil; toss well. Spoon over a crisp wedge of iceberg lettuce, making sure to use all the extra juices left in the bottom of the bowl.

29.

Broiled Eggplant with Miso-Walnut Vinaigrette

Toss with soba noodles or serve on a bed of greens.

Heat the broiler. Halve small eggplants lengthwise (or slice large ones) and rub them all over with vegetable oil and salt. While they're broiling, whisk together some miso, chopped walnuts, soy sauce, and rice vinegar. Cook the eggplant until it's browned and soft, then remove to a platter and pour the dressing over all. Garnish with chopped scallions.

30.

Duck Wraps with Plums

Fresh fruit updates Peking duck.

Buy roast duck and take the meat off the bones. Cut several ripe plums into wedges. Heat vegetable oil in a skillet and add some thinly sliced leeks (the white part only). When soft, add the duck and stir-fry for a minute or two, then add the plums, cooking and stirring until they're just warmed through. Roll in small flour tortillas or lettuce leaves, and serve with hoisin sauce for dipping.

31.

Summer Rolls with Barbecued Pork

An excellent use for any leftover meat or seafood.

Shred the pork and toss with a splash of fish sauce, some chiles, a squeeze of lime, and some chopped mint. Dip a sheet of rice paper into a bowl of hot water for about two seconds. Turn it and dip the piece you were holding in the water; lay on a damp towel. Put a little of the pork mixture at the bottom of the wrapper; roll and fold as you would a burrito. Serve with salted shredded cabbage tossed with sesame oil and rice vinegar.

32.

Sausage and Grape Bruschetta

Red grapes are prettier here.

Squeeze two Italian sausages from their casings and break the meat into a hot skillet with a little olive oil and a chopped red onion. Cook, stirring once in a while, until browned all over. Meanwhile, cut several thick slices of good Italian bread, brush with olive oil, and toast or broil until crisp outside but tender inside. When the sausage is done, stir in about a pound of grapes, mashing a bit to break some of them up. Cook until just warmed through. Top the bread with the sausage mixture and pan juices.

33.

Fish Tacos

Any firm white fish works well here; or try crab or shrimp.

Cook a chopped red onion in olive oil for a minute or two. When it's soft, add a big pinch of ground cumin or coriander and some salt and pepper. Keeping the heat relatively high, add a pound or so of fish fillets and stir to break them into chunks, cooking until they're just opaque. Off heat, squeeze lime juice over the mixture and scrape up any browned bits from the bottom of the pan. Warm corn tortillas and fill with the fish mixture. Top with shredded cabbage, chopped tomato or tomatillos, a splash of hot sauce, and a dollop of sour cream.

34.

Tuna-Anchovy Sandwich

You can use this to stuff celery sticks, too.

Mash olive oil–packed tuna with some anchovy fillets and minced garlic. Squeeze lemon juice over all and fold in some chopped black olives, halved cherry tomatoes, and chopped fresh basil or parsley. Spread on good crusty bread or serve with crisp lettuce cups for wrapping.

35.

Grilled Tomato Sandwich with Blue Cheese Spread

Thinly sliced roast beef will bulk this up considerably.

Mash blue cheese with a little softened cream cheese, chopped chives, and just enough milk to make it spreadable. Smear a thin layer on slices of good bread. Top with ripe tomato, salt, and pepper. Make sandwiches and slip into a buttered hot frying pan. (If you're making more than one sandwich, assemble them on a baking sheet and broil them on both sides.) Press down gently when you flip the sandwich and keep cooking until golden and gooey. Cut on the diagonal and serve with pickles or chow chow.

36.

Shrimp-Tomato-Arugula Wraps

Just what it sounds like.

Mince garlic and cook in vegetable oil till just fragrant, less than a minute. Add peeled shrimp and cook until pink, about three minutes more. Make a dressing of plain yogurt, lemon juice, chopped cilantro, salt, and pepper. Warm large flour tortillas (whole wheat are nice), then spread yogurt mixture on each tortilla and add arugula, sliced seeded tomato, the shrimp, and some lettuce. Roll tightly, cut in halves or quarters, and serve.

37.

Caramelized Caprese Sandwich

Halve good crusty rolls or squares of corn bread or focaccia and toast under the broiler. Slice ripe tomatoes crosswise into thick rounds; spread out on a broiler pan, drizzle with olive oil, sprinkle with salt and pepper, and quickly brown on both sides. Serve open-faced: bread first (olive bread is awesome), then sliced fresh mozzarella and fresh basil leaves, topped with the tomato slices; drizzle with pan juices.

38.

Portobello Burgers
with Tomato Mayonnaise

You can grill or broil the lettuce and tomato too, if you like.

Stem large portobellos; cut a large onion into thick slices. Brush both with oil and sprinkle with salt and pepper, then grill or broil until tender. Meanwhile, puree a large ripe, seeded tomato in a food processor with good-quality mayo, a clove of garlic, and a few fresh herb sprigs if you've got them handy. Halve rolls or buns, spread them with the mayonnaise, and fill with mushroom and onion, adding lettuce and more tomato. Serve.

39.

Grilled Fish Sandwich
with Chile-Lime-Carrot Relish

*Mayo scented with chile and lime is good as a dressing here too;
and use tomatoes if you can't find tomatillos.*

Grate two or three carrots and combine with lime juice, chili powder, minced garlic, salt, and pepper; press down to soften the carrots a bit. Brush any sturdy white fish with olive oil and grill until done, about three minutes per side. Split good-quality rolls; spread carrot relish on the bottom half and add sliced tomatillos, cilantro sprigs, and the fish.

40.

Five-Spice Lobster Sandwich

Or crab, or shrimp, or mixed seafood.

Combine a large pinch of five-spice powder with two tablespoons soy sauce, one tablespoon rice vinegar, and two teaspoons sesame oil. Add two chopped scallions, grated ginger, minced garlic, and minced fresh chile if you like. Mince a red bell pepper and add it to the dressing along with about two cups shredded cooked lobster. Mix well with a fork, taste, and add some salt and pepper. Spread on split baguette or rice cakes.

41.

Blackened Salmon Sandwich

Grind together some cumin seed, fennel seed, dried oregano, dried thyme, paprika, a little bit of cayenne, and salt; rub all over skinned salmon fillets. Heat a heavy skillet until almost smoking, add a film of oil, and cook salmon until well browned, about four minutes; then flip and cook until medium-done. Layer thickly sliced bread or rolls with thin-sliced onion, plain yogurt, arugula leaves, and salmon.

42.

Black Bean Tostada

In Mexico, this is called a clayuda.

Heat precooked or canned black beans, adding ground cumin, chili powder, fresh oregano, and salt. Shred cabbage and chop a few radishes or a chunk of jicama; grate some Mexican melting cheese like queso Oaxaca or cotija, and slice some smoked chorizo or other cooked sausage. Drain the beans and mash roughly. Lightly toast large tortillas under the broiler, then top with the beans, the cheese, and the meat. Return to the broiler to melt the cheese and serve, topped with the vegetables and a dollop of sour cream; put lime wedges on the side.

43.

Taco Slaw

Not your usual restaurant salad.

Load a big bowl up with shredded cabbage. Add precooked or canned drained pinto beans, a handful of corn kernels, lots of chopped tomatoes and red onions, sliced red bell pepper and avocado, bits of chopped smoked chorizo, and crumbled queso fresco. Break up some tortilla chips on top. Put a bunch of fresh cilantro in the blender with lime juice, olive oil, salt, pepper, and as much fresh or dried chile as you can stand. Give the mixture a good whirl, then use it to dress and toss the salad. Serve with crema for last-minute drizzling.

44.

Microwaved Honey Eggplant

Sort of amazing.

Combine a half cup each of chopped parsley and breadcrumbs with three tablespoons olive oil, two tablespoons honey, one minced garlic clove, and a pinch of salt. Cut one large or two medium eggplants crosswise into one-inch slices; then score the top of each slice. Put the slices in a dish and spread the breadcrumb mixture over the tops, pressing it into the slits. Partially cover with wax paper and microwave on high power for about five minutes. Remove the paper and cook another two or three minutes, until very soft. Sprinkle with lemon juice and serve with yogurt on the side.

45.

Balsamic Beef, Radicchio, and Romaine

Serve as a warm salad, or skip the lettuce and toss the beef mixture with pasta.

Shred a medium head of radicchio and a head of romaine lettuce. Brown about a half pound of ground beef in some olive oil with salt and pepper, then add a chopped red onion, a chopped garlic clove, and a chopped fresh red chile (or use a pinch of dried flakes). When the vegetables begin to get soft, add the radicchio, a splash of balsamic vinegar, and a little water. Cook until the radicchio is caramelized and the sauce thickens. Toss in a big bowl with the lettuce, adding more olive oil if needed; pass grated Parmesan at the table if you like.

46.

Swiss Chard with White Beans and Pancetta

Or bacon.

Dice a quarter pound of pancetta and sear in olive oil until golden and getting crisp. Meanwhile, take a large bunch of Swiss chard and chop, keeping stems and leaves separate. Add the stems to the pancetta; when they soften a bit, add the leaves. Stir until wilted, then add a quarter cup of raisins, a quarter cup of pine nuts, and a couple cups of precooked or canned navy beans (rinsed and drained). Warm until heated through and serve with toasted olive bread or toss with pasta.

47.

String Beans with Bacon and Tomatoes

Like stewed vegetables, only fresher.

Chop a fair amount of thick bacon and fry with some sliced onions in a deep skillet until the meat is cooked and the onions are soft. Pour off some of the fat if there's a lot; add string beans and cook and stir until brightly colored and beginning to soften. Stir in chopped ripe tomatoes and cook until just breaking apart. Garnish with chopped parsley and serve over white rice or thick slices of toast.

48.

Zucchini with Tomatoes and Chorizo

Serve on crusty bread or pasta.

Cut zucchini into quarter-inch disks; cook crumbled (Mexican) chorizo in olive oil for about three minutes, or until beginning to brown, then add diced shallot or onion and minced garlic; continue cooking until the shallot is translucent, a couple of minutes more. Add the zucchini and some chopped tomatoes; cover and cook until the zucchini is tender, about five more minutes. Add some lemon zest and juice, season with salt and pepper, and serve.

49.

Shrimp with Toasted Coconut

Great over a bed of jasmine rice.

Toast some shredded unsweetened coconut, shaking the pan to keep it from burning, until just golden; remove and set aside. Add some oil to the pan, along with peeled shrimp and some curry powder, and cook until the shrimp are pink. Add enough coconut milk to make the mixture saucy, along with some soy sauce and the toasted coconut. Serve garnished with fresh cilantro.

50.

Lettuce Wraps

Incredibly easy and impressive.

Toss good-quality shredded cooked chicken, cooked ground meat, or lump crabmeat with minced shallot or red onion, chopped cilantro, sesame oil, minced Thai chile, salt, and pepper. Take the large outer leaves from heads of Bibb or Boston lettuce, put a couple of tablespoons of the filling mixture in the middle of each leaf, then roll up like a burrito to eat.

51.

Grilled Vegetables with Quinoa

Don't hesitate to add leftover shredded chicken, crumbled sausage,
or even some fried tofu.

Heat the grill and cook the quinoa. Thread quartered shallots or red onions on one skewer, and cherry tomatoes and quartered mushrooms on another (they'll cook more quickly than the onions). Brush the vegetables with olive oil and sprinkle with salt and pepper. Grill the vegetables, turning as needed, until browned and done, about six minutes. Remove the vegetables from the skewers and toss them with the quinoa in large bowl; mix gently, season with more olive oil and salt and pepper as needed, garnish with freshly chopped basil, and serve.

52.

Black and Blue Tuna

Combine sushi-grade tuna steaks with a lot of grated ginger, some minced garlic, and a splash each of oil, soy sauce, fish sauce, and lime juice. Marinate about five minutes, then dredge in sesame seeds. For rare, sear each side for about two minutes on a hot grill or in a lightly oiled, well-seasoned pan. Slice and serve over a bed of watercress.

53.

Tuna with Pineapple, Cucumber, and Avocado

Try using toasted nori instead of lavash for the wrap.

Cut sushi-grade tuna into quarter-inch-thick slices; slice avocado and pineapple into pretty much equal-sized pieces. Very thinly slice a cucumber. Mix together minced ginger, lemon juice, soy sauce, and a little fish sauce. Lay cucumber slices on lavash or other wrap-type bread, overlapping them slightly, then top with the tuna, avocado, and pineapple; drizzle with the dressing, throw in a few sprigs of cilantro, and roll up.

54.

Grilled Fish Kebabs

Try any solid, meaty fish here.

Make a paste from a few cloves of garlic; salt; pepper; lemon juice; chopped fresh oregano, marjoram, or parsley; and olive oil. Cut fish into two-inch chunks, rub well with the paste, and thread onto skewers. Grill for about five minutes, turning as needed, until the fish is firm and slightly blackened. Serve with lemon wedges.

55.

Grilled Fish with Peach and Tomato Salad

Again, use whatever fish is fresh and firm.

Brush the fish with olive oil and season with salt and pepper. Slice an equal number of tomatoes and peaches and put them in a serving dish with diced red onion, chopped cilantro, olive oil, lime juice, salt, and pepper. Grill the fish, turning once, until just done, then serve with the salad and a slice of lemon or lime.

56.

Grilled Sardines with Summer Squash

Fresh sardines are fabulous on the grill.

Brush sardines (figure three or four per serving) with olive oil and sprinkle with salt, pepper, and freshly chopped oregano. Slice zucchini and yellow summer squash into half-inch-thick pieces. Brush the squash with olive oil and sprinkle with salt and pepper. Grill the squash until it's softening, about four minutes per side. Grill the sardines a little less, two or three minutes per side. Serve the sardines over a bed of alternating green and yellow squash, with lots of lemon wedges on the side.

57.

Grilled Fish with Spinach and Tomatoes

Use any white-fleshed fish fillets or steaks here.

Brush the fillets with olive oil and season them with salt and pepper; grill until done. Meanwhile, cook a couple of cloves of garlic in olive oil until fragrant, then add spinach and keep cooking until just wilted, just a couple of minutes; sprinkle with salt and pepper. Thinly slice a couple of tomatoes, and layer on plates; drizzle with olive oil. Top with the spinach and fish and serve with lemon.

58.

Scallop and Peach Ceviche

Plums and pineapple are also terrific here.

Dice high-quality scallops and peaches into equal-sized cubes about a quarter- to a half-inch square. Toss them together in a bowl, along with finely diced red onion, finely chopped tarragon, lots of lime juice (the acid in the lime juice will "cook" the scallops in a few minutes), salt, and pepper. Adjust the seasonings and serve.

59.

Grilled Fish
with Raw Pineapple Chutney

Any sturdy, meaty fish will work.

Combine diced pineapple with chopped scallions, chopped cilantro, salt, pepper, lime juice, and a little cayenne. Brush the fish with olive oil and season with salt and pepper and a squeeze of lime juice. Grill the fish until done. Serve topped with a couple of spoonfuls of the chutney.

60.

Braised Fish with Cherry Tomatoes

A lovely summer dinner served with good bread and a crisp salad.

Cut cherry tomatoes into halves. Sprinkle them and some sturdy white fish steaks or fillets with salt, pepper, and fresh or dried oregano. Heat some olive oil and add the fish; cook until it begins to brown, then turn and add a cup of not-too-dry white wine, some minced garlic, and the tomatoes. Bring to a simmer and cook until the fish is done (a thin-bladed knife inserted into its center will meet little resistance). Serve in soup bowls with the broth.

61.

Grilled Watermelon
and Shrimp Skewers

Nice with basmati rice mixed with toasted coconut.

Light a charcoal or gas grill. Alternate chunks of watermelon and large shrimp on skewers; brush with olive oil and sprinkle with curry powder, salt, and pepper. Grill, turning as needed, until the shrimp is opaque. Garnish with chopped scallions and pistachios and serve with lime wedges.

62.

Crab Cake Burger

*Dredging the patties in breadcrumbs instead of mixing them
with the crab makes for a fantastically crisp crust.*

Combine about a pound of crabmeat with a few tablespoons of mayonnaise, a tablespoon of Dijon mustard, a couple of tablespoons of freshly chopped parsley, salt, and pepper; form into patties. Gently coat the patties in fresh breadcrumbs and sear in hot oil. Cook the patties until they're just golden, turning once. Serve on good-quality buns or rolls topped with lettuce and tomato if you like; garnish with slices of lemon.

63.

Shrimp with Cilantro, Garlic, and Lime

Serve alone, over noodles or rice, or even as part of a salad.

In a large bowl, combine a handful or so of chopped cilantro, some minced garlic, the zest and juice of a lime, a tablespoon of fish sauce, salt, and pepper. In vegetable oil, cook a pound of shrimp until pink and no longer translucent, three or four minutes. (Or use squid; cook it for even less time.) Toss the shrimp in the cilantro mixture and serve.

64.

Shrimp, Scallop,
and Cherry Tomato Kebabs

Use chunks of firm fish here too, if you like.

Skewer shrimp, scallops, and cherry tomatoes, alternating fish and tomatoes. Brush with olive oil and sprinkle with salt and pepper. Grill the kebabs until the fish is done and the tomatoes are soft and slightly blackened, turning as needed. Sprinkle with chopped parsley (or a mixture of parsley and minced onion) and serve with lemon.

65.

Bacon-Wrapped Scallops

Modernizing an old fave.

In a pan, cook the bacon until it's pliable and golden, about five minutes; drain on paper towels and set aside. Season the scallops with salt and pepper, wrap each in a half-slice of bacon, and secure with a toothpick; sear the bundles, turning once, until the scallops are opaque and the bacon is nicely browned, about five minutes total. Dress greens lightly with olive oil and fresh lemon juice and serve the scallops on top.

66.

Stir-Fried Corn and Clams

Fun to eat with chopsticks or your hands.

Cut ears of corn crosswise into one-inch slices. Put a film of vegetable oil in the bottom of a large skillet over medium-high heat. Add some ginger and garlic and the corn and cook and stir until coated and beginning to color, just a minute or two. Add scrubbed clams, a splash each of water and white wine or sherry, and a handful of fermented black beans; cover and cook until the clams open. Taste and adjust the seasoning and serve, garnished with chopped scallions or cilantro and lime wedges.

67.

Grilled Lemon-Tarragon Chicken

Tarragon and chicken are a classic and wonderful marriage.

Mix the zest of a lemon with some chopped fresh tarragon (no more than a teaspoon or so; it's strong). Brush thin chicken breasts with olive oil, smear with the zest and tarragon, and season with salt and pepper. Grill the chicken, turning it once, until cooked through. Squeeze more lemon juice over the chicken, then serve, with coarse-grain mustard on the side.

68.

Grilled Chicken Kebabs

It takes just a couple of minutes more to slice up some eggplant
and zucchini and throw them onto the grill with the kebabs.

Cut boneless chicken breasts or thighs into chunks. Combine a teaspoon of paprika, a teaspoon of cinnamon, a dash of nutmeg, salt, and pepper together in a small bowl. Toss the chicken with a few tablespoons of olive oil and some fresh lemon juice; sprinkle well with the spice mixture. Thread the chicken onto skewers and grill until done, then serve with lemon wedges.

69.

Grilled Chicken Paillards
with Endive and Radicchio

The grilled lemons make this spectacular.

Pound chicken breasts to quarter-inch thickness, brush them with olive oil, and season with salt and pepper. Cut the endive and radicchio into halves, brush the cut side with olive oil, and season with salt and pepper. Cut three or four lemons in half and brush the cut side with olive oil. On a hot grill, cook the chicken, turning it once, until it's brown and done, about three minutes per side; cook the endive, radicchio, and lemons, cut side down, until browned, about four minutes. Serve the chicken with the vegetables, squeezing the grilled lemon over everything.

70.

Jerk Chicken

Serve with black beans and rice or couscous.

In a food processor, combine a half cup of white vinegar, two tablespoons of rum, one or two habanero chiles, a red onion, one tablespoon of dried thyme, two teaspoons of salt, one teaspoon of cracked black peppercorns, one tablespoon each of allspice, cinnamon, and ginger, and two teaspoons of molasses. Process until smooth. Cover a pound of boneless chicken (thighs or breasts) in this mixture and let sit for about five minutes (or up to an hour). Grill the chicken, turning once, until browned and cooked through.

71.

Chicken with Chinese Long Beans and Lemongrass

If you can't find Chinese long beans, use regular green beans.

Cut Chinese long beans into one-inch pieces; cook in boiling, salted water until crisp-tender, about two minutes. Drain and shock in ice water; set aside. Soften a diced onion in a little oil, along with some minced garlic, for about a minute; remove. Stir-fry a pound of chicken that's been cut into half-inch strips until the chicken turns white and is partially cooked, about three minutes. Add a tablespoon of minced lemongrass (the tender inner part only), a tablespoon of fish sauce, a teaspoon of ground coriander, a cup of chicken stock, and about two tablespoons of oyster sauce; mix well and continue cooking until the chicken is done, about three more minutes. Add the green beans, the onion, and garlic and toss well so that everything is coated in the sauce. Season with salt and lots of pepper and serve.

72.

Spicy Chicken Tacos with Chipotle Cream

Chipotles are hot, so use them to taste.

Mix a cup of sour cream with diced canned chipotles, along with a little of their sauce (adobo). Combine two tablespoons of brown sugar, a tablespoon each of paprika and chili powder, salt, and pepper in a small bowl. Pound chicken breasts to half-inch thickness, brush them with oil, and coat them with the spice rub. Grill or broil the chicken, turning once, until it's cooked through, about six minutes; meanwhile, dice a tomato, an avocado, and a red onion. Slice the chicken and serve it on warm corn tortillas with the vegetables, and chipotle cream; garnish with cilantro.

73.

Spiced Chicken with Mango Salsa

I grill this chicken, but you can just as easily cook it quickly in a pan with a bit of oil or butter.

Heat a grill or grill pan. In a small bowl, mix one teaspoon each of cinnamon, cumin, and paprika; a pinch of cayenne; salt; and pepper. Rub quarter-inch-thick chicken cutlets with the spice mix. In another bowl, combine a chopped mango, half a diced red onion, a handful of chopped cilantro, the juice of half a lime, a tablespoon of olive oil, salt, and pepper. Grill the chicken, turning once, until well browned and cooked through. Serve the chicken topped with mango salsa and lime wedges.

74·

Pork Paillards with Grilled Pineapple

Pound boneless pork chops or medallions cut from the tenderloin to quarter-inch thickness; slice a pineapple into half-inch rings. Brush both with olive oil and season with salt and pepper. Grill the pineapple until it's well browned on both sides, about four minutes. Grill the pork until it's cooked through, about two minutes on each side. Serve the pork and pineapple with a good steak sauce.

75·

Grilled Pork Skewers with Worcestershire

Mix a quarter cup of Worcestershire sauce with two teaspoons of lime juice. Slice a lime into eight wedges. Cut pork tenderloin into one-inch cubes, brush with the Worcestershire mixture, and sprinkle with salt and pepper. Thread the pork and lime wedges alternately on skewers. Grill the pork, turning as needed to slightly blacken on all sides and brushing repeatedly with the sauce, until cooked through. Serve, squeezing the grilled lime over the pork.

76.

Spicy Grilled Pork with Peach Marmalade

If you like sweet and savory combos, you'll love this.

Combine a quarter cup of peach (or apricot) preserves with some minced garlic, a tablespoon of olive oil, a tablespoon of soy sauce, a half teaspoon of dry mustard, a pinch of cayenne pepper, and salt. Coat thin, boneless pork chops with the marmalade and grill, taking care not to let the marmalade burn. Slice fresh peaches (or apricots) in half, and remove the pits; sprinkle with salt and grill flesh-side down for a couple of minutes until colored and just softening. Serve the pork with the grilled fruit.

77.

Grilled Pork with Basil Peanut Sauce

Use natural peanut butter, please (peanuts and salt, nothing else).

In a blender, combine a few handfuls of fresh basil, a lump of peanut butter (say, a quarter cup), a tablespoon or two of fish sauce, a clove of garlic, a small piece of fresh ginger, a pinch of red chile flakes, and a little water; process until you have a smooth, thick paste, then taste and add more of whatever you like. Rub the paste over a pound of boneless pork chops (about a half-inch thick) and set aside to marinate for a few minutes. Slice a couple of heads of baby bok choy in half; brush them with peanut or sesame oil and sprinkle with salt, pepper, and lime juice. Grill the pork until it's slightly blackened and cooked through; grill the bok choy until it wilts slightly and is tender when pierced with a knife. Serve together.

78.

Grilled Steaks with Rosemary Plums

Don't bother to skewer the fruit if you're feeling lazy;
just lay the rosemary on top as the pieces cook.

Brush rib eye, strip, or sirloin steaks with olive oil and sprinkle with salt and pepper. Cut plums into quarters, remove the pits, and skewer them on rosemary sprigs. Grill everything, turning once, until the steaks are just done—five minutes or so, depending on their thickness—and the plums are soft and slightly blackened. Serve together, with garlic bread.

79.

Korean Barbecued Beef

Traditionally eaten with white rice, wrapped in lettuce leaves.

Slice a flank (or better: skirt) steak into half-inch pieces. Mix together one teaspoon of sesame oil, one tablespoon of brown sugar, three tablespoons of soy sauce, one tablespoon of mirin (or a little honey mixed with water), two minced cloves of garlic, and a pinch of red chile flakes. Brush the meat with the sauce and grill until it begins to crisp, about two minutes per side, basting frequently. Serve the beef sprinkled with toasted sesame seeds and chopped scallions.

80.

Grilled Skirt Steak with Tomatillo Salsa

Use tomatoes, peaches, or pineapple here.

Season a skirt steak with salt and pepper. In a food processor, puree three or four tomatillos, a handful of cilantro, a clove of garlic, a jalapeño or other green chile, a couple of tablespoons of olive oil, some lemon or lime juice, a dash of sugar, salt, and pepper; process until smooth, then taste and adjust the seasonings. Grill the steak to medium-rare, about three minutes on each side. Serve the steak sliced against the grain and drizzled with the salsa.

81.

A Very Good Burger

In a food processor, coarsely grind a pound or so of sirloin or chuck, cut in chunks, with half of a white onion. Season the meat mixture generously with salt and pepper, and form it into patties, handling it as little as possible. Grill the burgers on each side for about three minutes for rare, and a minute more for each further degree of doneness. Serve on buns or rolls with freshly sliced tomatoes, pickles, lettuce, bacon, avocado, or whatever you like.

82.

Hot-and-Sour Beef and Okra Stir-fry

High heat minimizes okra's slime factor.

Trim okra and cut in half lengthwise. Put a film of vegetable oil in the bottom of a large skillet set over high heat. When hot, add the okra, sprinkle with salt and pepper, and cook without stirring until it sputters and browns a bit; stir and let it go a minute or two more. Meanwhile, cut a sirloin or flank steak into strips and chop up some garlic, ginger, onions, and fresh hot chile. Remove the okra from the pan, adding more oil if needed. Stir-fry the beef until almost done; then add the aromatics and chile and sprinkle lightly with sugar. Splash some rice vinegar and soy sauce in the pan to make a little sauce. Add the okra and some cilantro or Thai basil and give a good stir. Serve over rice.

83.

Grilled Lamb Chops
with Lemony Yogurt Sauce

*This is a lovely sauce whose flavor profile you can readily change by replacing the spices
with chopped dill or mint.*

Combine a cup of plain yogurt with a few tablespoons of lemon juice, a quarter cup of diced cucumber, and a teaspoon or so of ground cumin and paprika (or pimentón). Season the chops with salt and pepper; grill until medium-rare, about three minutes per side depending on thickness. Serve the lamb with the yogurt sauce.

84.

Grilled Lamb Chops
with Summer Fruit

Grill whatever's in season—nectarines, plums, peaches, and pears are all delicious.

Season lamb chops with salt, pepper, and a sprinkle of cinnamon; cut the fruit into quarters. Cook the lamb chops, turning once, until medium-rare (timing will depend on how thick the chops are). While the lamb is cooking, add the fruit to the grill and cook until it begins to soften and you have nice grill marks. Serve the lamb topped with the grilled fruit.

85.

Shrimp and Pasta with Pesto

You can always use store-bought pesto; but I wouldn't.

Boil salted water for pasta and cook it. Meanwhile, in a food processor, puree a few large handfuls of fresh basil, a large handful of freshly grated Parmesan, and a small one of pine nuts or walnuts; and salt, pepper, and enough olive oil to reach a smooth consistency—you don't want the pesto too thin. In some olive oil cook about a half pound of small whole or large chopped shrimp. Drain the pasta, reserving some of the cooking water, and toss it with the pesto and shrimp, using some of the pasta water to moisten the mixture if needed. Serve warm or cold.

86.

Pasta with Cherry Tomatoes

This is sublime when summer tomatoes are at their peak.

Boil salted water for pasta and cook it; meanwhile, cook a minced clove of garlic in olive oil for a couple of minutes, until fragrant. Add about a pound of whole cherry or grape tomatoes to the pan and cook over low heat. When a few have burst, turn off the heat. Drain the pasta and toss it gently with the tomatoes. Season with salt and lots of freshly ground pepper; serve with freshly chopped basil and/or freshly grated Parmesan.

87.

Pasta Salad with Beans and Herbs

Serve as a room-temperature salad, or warm as a main course.

Cook cut pasta, like ziti, then drain and rinse. Meanwhile, combine a couple of minced shallots; some drained precooked or canned kidney, garbanzo, and black beans; a few tablespoons of olive oil; some minced garlic; a teaspoon of red chile flakes; and lots of freshly chopped parsley, along with (if you have it) a little dill, mint, and basil. (Add some chopped or cherry tomatoes if you like.) Toss the pasta with the bean mixture and season well with salt and pepper.

88.

Pasta with Spicy Squid

Fastest, of course, with pre-cleaned squid.

Boil salted water for pasta and cook it. Meanwhile, slice fresh squid into rings; cook some minced garlic and a diced red chile in olive oil. Add a splash of dry white wine to the pan and bring to a boil. Reduce the heat and add the squid; cook until just done, about two minutes. Toss in the drained pasta, adding extra olive oil if needed, and season well with salt and pepper, and perhaps a little bit of red chile flakes, before serving.

89.

Cellophane Noodles with Shrimp and Papaya

Add some mango or pineapple, or substitute one for the papaya if you like.

Soak the cellophane noodles in boiling water until tender, rinse, and drain. Peel a papaya and dice it into quarter-inch pieces; thinly slice a few scallions; chop a handful of fresh basil; and mince a Thai (or another) chile. Combine in a bowl with a pound of cooked shrimp. Whisk together a few tablespoons of rice wine vinegar, a teaspoon of sugar, and a pinch of salt; then combine with the shrimp mixture and the noodles. Garnish with chopped peanuts and cilantro, mint, or more basil.

90.

Pasta with Spicy Shellfish

This works with peeled shrimp, squid, or crabmeat or shucked clams, oysters, or mussels.

Boil salted water for pasta and cook it; meanwhile, soften a couple of minced garlic cloves and a pinch of red chile flakes in some olive oil; cook until fragrant, about two minutes. Add about a pound of fresh seafood to the garlic and chile flakes, and continue cooking until the fish is cooked (or in the case of crab, warmed through), anywhere from three to five more minutes. Toss the pasta with the seafood, along with a bit of the pasta cooking water if needed. Drizzle with more olive oil if you like; season with salt, pepper, and more red chile flakes if necessary; and garnish with freshly chopped basil or parsley.

91.

Pasta with Puttanesca Cruda

Boil salted water for pasta and cook it; meanwhile, in a large bowl, mix together two large chopped tomatoes, a handful of pitted and chopped olives (any kind, as long as they're good), a couple of tablespoons of drained capers, a handful each of chopped fresh basil and parsley, several chopped anchovy fillets, a little minced garlic, a pinch of red chile flakes, and about a quarter cup of olive oil. Toss the hot pasta and about a quarter cup of the cooking liquid with the tomato mixture, adding more cooking liquid if necessary. Season with salt and pepper, and garnish with more chopped herbs.

92.

Poached Tofu with Broccoli

Bring a large pot of water to a boil and salt it. Lower a brick of firm tofu into the water and cook until it just floats, five to 10 minutes. Meanwhile, whisk together equal parts soy sauce, sake, lemon and orange juices, and water with a little sugar and a few drops of sesame oil; break a head of broccoli into florets. When you remove the tofu, plunge the broccoli into the pot; count to 20 and then drain. Serve thick slices of the tofu with the florets, drizzling the dressing over all. Sprinkle with panko too, if you like.

93.

Blueberry Ricotta Cheesecakes

One of my favorite ways to make the most of fresh blueberries.

In a food processor, finely grind one sleeve of graham crackers. Combine the crackers with about three tablespoons of melted butter and press the mixture into ramekins. Whisk a cup of ricotta cheese with a cup of cream cheese (an eight-ounce package), a couple of tablespoons of honey, the zest and juice of a lemon, and a pinch of salt. Spread the ricotta mixture evenly in the prepared crust, top with lots of fresh blueberries, and serve, or refrigerate for up to a day before serving.

94.

Apricot Cream Upside-Down Pie

Equally good with fresh or dried apricots.

Halve and pit a pound of apricots; put them in a pan with a half cup of brandy and bring to a boil. Continue cooking until the apricots break down, about eight minutes. Whip a cup of cream, along with a tablespoon of brandy, until thick. In a food processor, pulse about eight graham crackers with a good handful of pistachios (pecans are nice here too), leaving the mixture slightly chunky. When the apricots are done, fold them into the whipped cream. Serve a heaping spoonful of the apricot cream in a bowl sprinkled with the graham cracker–nut crunch on top.

95.

Frozen Hot Chocolate

Serve this with biscotti or other not-too-sweet cookies.

Melt six ounces of good dark chocolate with a quarter cup of cream or half-and-half, being careful not to boil. Once the chocolate is melted, taste and add a little sugar if you like. Put it in the blender with three cups of ice and pulse until an even consistency is reached. Serve in small bowls or cups.

96.

Ginger-Lemon "Ice Cream"

Add more candied ginger if you like.

In a food processor, puree two tablespoons of fresh ginger, peeled and roughly chopped, with a half cup of sugar, two cups of cream, and the juice and zest of one lemon. Add ice, pulsing, and pushing down as necessary, until thick and icy; add a couple of tablespoons of chopped candied ginger at the end and process until just combined. Serve immediately, or freeze for up to several days.

97.

Peach Lemon "Cheesecake"

This works just as well with nectarines, raspberries, strawberries, or even mangoes.

Puree two peaches with the juice of one lemon, two tablespoons of sugar, and about six ounces of goat cheese—you want a nice thick mixture, so use more cheese as needed. Spoon the mixture into individual ramekins, smooth the top, and cover with a layer of chopped pistachios. Sprinkle the nuts with powdered sugar and a drizzle of honey.

98.

Fresh Fruit Gratin

Use stone fruits (peaches, nectarines, plums, or apricots) or berries.

Wash, pit, and prepare the fruit as needed; heat the broiler. Combine one cup of sour cream with about two tablespoons of sugar and one teaspoon of vanilla. Put two to three cups of fruit in a baking dish just large enough to hold it, top with the sour cream mixture, and sprinkle with a teaspoon of sugar; broil for about two minutes, or until the cream begins to brown.

99.

Blackberries with Champagne and Tarragon

Oddly appealing.

Finely chop a couple of teaspoons of fresh tarragon. Toss a quart of rinsed blackberries with a few tablespoons of sugar, a cup or so of sparkling wine, and the tarragon. Let the mixture sit for about five minutes, or longer if you have time, and serve in small bowls with your favorite sugar cookie.

100.

Ice Cream Sandwich

Use different flavors of ice cream or sorbet, or vary the jam (or skip it altogether).

Let vanilla ice cream soften for five minutes. Lay cocoa snaps or gingersnaps (or vanilla wafers) out in two rows and spread raspberry jam thinly on each one. Add a scoop of the softened ice cream to half the cookies and top with the remaining cookies to make sandwiches.

101.

Quick Summer Fruit Ice Cream

All you need is a food processor.

Freeze a pound of fresh sliced fruit (trimmed, seeded, or pitted as needed). When hard, put in the machine along with one-half cup crème fraîche (or yogurt or silken tofu for that matter). Add as much or as little sugar as you like and just enough water, a spoonful at a time, to let the processor do its thing. Scrape down the bowl as needed; but don't overprocess, or the ice cream will liquefy. Serve immediately; or if you freeze for later, let it sit out for 10 or 15 minutes to soften a bit.

FALL

Much of summer's bounty remains

through early fall, and as it starts to dwindle, it's replaced by the late-harvest fruits and vegetables that will carry through the winter—apples, pears, winter squash, and a return of many of the cool-weather vegetables of spring. The combination of grilling and braising, of summer and winter, makes this a magical time to cook, and one with more options than any other.

1.

Spicy Escarole with Croutons and Eggs

You might add a bit of dried oregano, or garlic, or both to the croutons before toasting.

Cut good-quality bread into one-inch cubes; toss the bread with two tablespoons of olive oil, salt, and pepper and toast them until golden, about three or four minutes. Cook a bunch of chopped escarole in two tablespoons of butter for about five minutes, or until wilted. Toss the escarole with the croutons, a pinch or two of red chile flakes, freshly squeezed lemon juice, olive oil, and freshly grated Parmesan cheese. Serve the greens and croutons in bowls with a soft-boiled or poached egg on top, along with more Parmesan.

2.

Mediterranean Poached Eggs

This is fine when the eggs are scrambled, too.

Slice a cup or so of mushrooms and a handful of black olives; chop an onion and two or three plum tomatoes. In a couple of tablespoons of olive oil, cook a smashed clove of garlic and the onion for about two minutes. Add the olives, mushrooms, and tomatoes and let the mixture simmer over medium heat. Poach four eggs and toast thick slices of peasant bread. Add a handful of chopped fresh basil and a couple of tablespoons of capers to the vegetable mixture; season with salt and pepper. Serve the vegetables and eggs on the bread, with lemon wedges on the side.

3.

Egg and Carrot Cake with Soy

Made with common ingredients, but unusual and delicious.

Grate a large carrot while you melt a tablespoon of butter in a skillet over medium heat; add the grated carrot and some minced garlic. Whisk four eggs with a couple of tablespoons of milk in a bowl and add them to the carrots; cook as you would a frittata. When the eggs are almost set, add a few dashes of soy sauce and a sprinkle of scallions and serve. (Good at room temperature, too.)

4.

Huevos Rancheros

For a less conventional version, replace the tomatoes in the salsa with peaches or pineapple.

Chop two large tomatoes, half a red onion, a small chile, and a handful of fresh cilantro; mix together with freshly squeezed lime juice, salt, and pepper. Warm a can of black beans (if you have homemade, all the better). While the beans are warming, make eggs any way you like: fried, poached, or scrambled. Top a warm tortilla with some beans, the eggs, and the salsa; garnish with fresh avocado and more cilantro.

5.

Breakfast Burritos

Basically a tortilla filled with eggs and other stuff.

Heat a can of black, red, or refried beans (or use homemade). Warm large flour tortillas in the oven, in the microwave, or in a dry skillet until just soft. Scramble a couple of eggs and cook them to the desired doneness. Spread some beans down the middle of a tortilla, top with grated cheese, eggs, and then anything else you like: olives, scallions, avocado, tomatoes, cilantro, bacon, sausage, salsa—you get the picture. Fold the short sides of the tortillas in, roll lengthwise, and serve.

6.

Brunch Baked Eggs

Really substantial.

Heat the oven to 400°F. In a pan over medium-high heat, melt a tablespoon or two of butter. Add a bunch of chopped spinach; cover the pan and let the spinach wilt. Add a half cup of cream, a cup of ricotta cheese, a handful of grated provolone, a couple of tablespoons of cognac (optional), salt, pepper, and a sprinkle of nutmeg. Bring this mixture to a simmer, stirring often, for about two more minutes. Divide the spinach mixture among four oven-safe bowls or ramekins (or cook in one big bowl); crack an egg over the top of each. Put the bowls on a cookie sheet and bake them for eight to 10 minutes, or until the whites of the eggs are just set. Serve with toasted bread.

7.

In-Shell Clam Chowder

A rustic spin on the classic.

Heat some olive oil in a pot, and cook a chopped onion for a couple of minutes until soft. Stir in some chopped celery, four cups of fish or clam broth (or water), and a cup each of heavy cream and dry white wine; add a few thyme sprigs, and a pound of potatoes, cut into quarter-inch dice. Bring to a boil, then reduce the heat to medium and cook until the potatoes are tender, about 10 minutes. Add a couple dozen scrubbed clams, season well with salt and pepper, and cover and cook until the clams pop open, just a couple of minutes more. Serve in shallow bowls, garnished with chopped parsley and lemon wedges.

8.

Mushroom and Nori Soup

Light, delicate, flavorful, and unusual.

In a pot over high heat, cook about three cups of mushrooms (any combination works; oyster and shiitake is especially good) in a couple of tablespoons of butter until they begin to release their liquid; add a diced onion, a minced garlic clove, and a chopped celery stalk and cook until the onion is translucent. Add about four cups of vegetable or chicken stock, a quarter cup of soy sauce, the juice of a lemon, a pinch of celery seed, salt, and pepper. Cook until the vegetables are tender. Tear or slice a sheet of nori into strips and put in soup bowls; pour soup over the nori (it will mostly dissolve) and serve.

9.

Lemony Red Lentil Soup with Cilantro

Red lentils cook very quickly, but allow more time if you substitute any other type.

Cook a chopped onion in olive oil in a saucepan until soft; add one cup of red lentils and four cups of chicken broth and bring to a boil; continue simmering until the lentils are soft. Puree a handful of cilantro with a few tablespoons of olive oil and a pinch of salt; set aside. If you like, puree half the lentils until almost smooth; return them to the pan. Add about two tablespoons of lemon juice or more to taste. Stir in the cilantro puree, adjust the seasonings, and serve with crusty bread or a mound of rice in the center.

10.

Egg Drop Soup

Nothing could be easier.

Bring a quart of stock (chicken or vegetable) to a slow bubble; gently pour four beaten eggs into the stock while stirring. Add soy sauce to taste and garnish with some chopped cilantro or scallions; a little sesame oil is nice, too.

Curried Coconut–Butternut Squash Soup

You can buy pre-peeled, precut squash, and just cut it down to quarter-inch pieces.

Cook two cups of chopped squash in a few tablespoons of vegetable oil, along with a diced onion, a teaspoon of cumin, a half teaspoon of cinnamon, and a teaspoon of curry powder (or more to taste). Cook the vegetables and spices until the onion is soft, about three minutes. Add five cups of chicken broth or water and a cup of coconut milk; bring to a boil and cook for about six minutes or until the squash is tender and easily pierced with a knife. Serve the soup topped with fresh cilantro and crusty bread or a scoop of rice.

Tomato Soup with Chickpeas and Greens

Fresh tomatoes and dried chickpeas cooked by you make this even better.

Drain a can of diced tomatoes and a can of chickpeas (if you cooked the chickpeas yourself, use some of their broth in the soup). Cook a diced onion, a diced carrot, and a diced stalk of celery in olive oil until soft. Add one crushed clove of garlic, the tomatoes, the beans, and about four cups of chicken or vegetable broth. Bring to a boil; add a bunch of chopped chard or beet greens (or spinach), reduce to a simmer, and cook for five more minutes. Meanwhile, brush sliced baguette or another good bread with olive oil, and toast. Serve soup with croutons on top.

13.

Broccoli Rabe and Garlic Soup

Some crushed dried chile flakes are nice here.

In a 450°F oven, roast a handful of smashed garlic cloves with a little olive oil for about five minutes. Bring about six cups of stock to a boil; add the garlic, stir in about a half cup of orzo or other small pasta, and a bunch of chopped broccoli rabe; continue cooking until the pasta and rabe are tender. Add lemon juice to taste, along with some salt and pepper. Serve, garnished with freshly grated Parmesan cheese if you like.

14.

Cream of Turnip Soup

This can be rich and creamy, or light and brothy.

Soften half a chopped onion in a couple of tablespoons of butter in a pot over medium heat, along with a smashed clove of garlic, two or three chopped white turnips, and a pinch of salt, for three to five minutes. Add six cups of hot broth, a quarter cup of cream, one bay leaf, and a teaspoon of tarragon, and bring to a boil. Simmer and cook until the turnips are tender, about five minutes. Add a cup of chopped turnip or other greens, stir until they wilt, and serve.

15.

Chile Sweet Potato Soup

Peel about a pound of sweet potatoes and grate or mince them in the food processor. Cook a couple minced cloves of garlic, some diced onion, and a chopped fresh chile in some olive oil until tender; stir in the sweet potatoes and add enough water to cover by about an inch. Bring to a boil, then lower the heat to a vigorous simmer, partially cover, and cook, stirring occasionally, until the sweet potatoes are tender. Stir in some fresh or dried sage and season with salt and pepper. Puree if you like, then add a splash of cream, heat through, and serve with croutons.

16.

Seafood Ramen

Shrimp, calamari, and scallops complement each other beautifully,
but you can use any combination of seafood you like here.

Soak rice noodles in boiling water until tender (two to five minutes, depending on their size), drain, and set aside. Bring four cups of fish, chicken, or other stock and two cups of coconut milk to a boil. Add a pound of seafood to the pot along with a smashed clove of garlic, a handful of chopped scallions, a few dashes of fish sauce, and a thinly sliced hot red pepper. Continue cooking until the fish is done, about three minutes. Divide the noodles among bowls and ladle the soup over the noodles; serve topped with chopped cilantro and a squeeze of lime juice.

17.

Udon Noodle and Miso Soup with Fresh Shiitake Mushrooms

Make this heartier by adding a pound of seafood,
sliced chicken breast or tofu, or thinly sliced beef.

Cook the udon noodles. Bring six cups of vegetable, mushroom, or chicken stock to a boil. Put one-third cup of miso in a bowl and add a ladleful of hot stock to it; whisk until smooth. Add the miso to the stock, along with three cups of sliced shiitake mushroom caps. Cook for about five minutes, then add the drained noodles, garnish with chopped scallions, and serve.

18.

Spinach Salad with Oranges and Goat Cheese

An instant favorite.

Heat the broiler. Finely chop a handful of pecans. Cut a log of goat cheese into half-inch disks; gently pat pecans on all sides of the goat cheese rounds and put them on a greased baking sheet. Broil on both sides until browned and warm, just a couple minutes. Peel two large oranges and separate into sections; thinly slice a small red onion. Whisk together about a quarter cup of olive oil, a few tablespoons of fresh orange juice, a teaspoon or so of mustard, salt, and pepper. In a large bowl, combine a big mound of well-washed spinach, the onion, and the orange slices; toss everything with the dressing and serve topped with a warm disk of pecan-crusted goat cheese.

19.

Endive and Warm Pear Salad with Stilton

Any good blue cheese can take the place of the Stilton here.

Cut three or four pears into eighths; toss them with a couple of tablespoons of olive oil, along with some salt and pepper. Thinly slice a shallot. Cook the pears and shallot in a skillet over medium-high heat until the pears are browning and the shallot slices are wilted; add a tablespoon of maple syrup during the last 30 seconds or so of cooking. Toss the warm pan mixture, and any remaining juices, in a bowl with endive and watercress (or any other greens you like), along with more olive oil and a bit of sherry vinegar. Garnish with crumbled Stilton and serve.

20.

Greek-Style Eggplant Salad

Peeling the eggplant isn't necessary unless the skin is thick and tough.

Heat a broiler or grill (you can use a grill pan, but you'll have to work in batches). Slice an eggplant into quarter-inch rounds; brush with olive oil and sprinkle with salt. Broil or grill until seared on both sides and soft in the center, about five minutes. Thinly slice a small red onion. Put the eggplant, onion slices, crumbled feta cheese, a handful of pitted black olives (oil-cured are good here), and chopped fresh oregano in a bowl. Drizzle with olive oil and season with salt and pepper and serve over greens along with a big squeeze of lemon.

21.

Salad Lyonnaise

A classic.

Bring a pot of water to a gentle boil. Cut bacon or pancetta into small pieces, fry until crisp, and set aside. In a small bowl, combine about a quarter cup of olive oil, a couple of tablespoons of red wine vinegar, a teaspoon of Dijon mustard, salt, and pepper. Crack eggs into the boiling water and poach them for about three minutes, or until set on the outside but still runny on the inside. Remove the eggs with a slotted spoon and drain completely. Toss a few handfuls of frisée or romaine with the bacon and the dressing and serve with a poached egg on top.

22.

Tofu Salad

If you like egg salad, try this.

In a large bowl, whisk together mayonnaise, mustard, soy sauce, and rice wine vinegar with some salt and pepper. Stir in chopped scallions, celery, red bell pepper, and some fresh minced chile if you like. Use your fingers to crumble firm tofu into the bowl and toss with a fork to combine and mash, adding more dressing ingredients if the mixture seems too dry. Serve the salad on a bed of watercress or Bibb lettuce, or rolled up in warmed whole wheat flour tortillas.

23.

Hummus with Pita

There is really no reason to ever buy hummus; homemade is undeniably better, even if you start with canned chickpeas.

Drain a can of chickpeas (or cook some) and reserve the liquid. In a food processor, puree the chickpeas with a few tablespoons of olive oil, a couple of tablespoons of tahini (optional), a large clove of garlic (more or less), a few tablespoons of freshly squeezed lemon juice, and about a teaspoon of cumin, along with salt and pepper. Slowly add chickpea liquid—or water or more oil—until you have a smooth puree; adjust the seasonings. Serve on toasted pita, drizzled with more olive oil and sprinkled with paprika.

24.

Tuna Sandwich with Fennel
and Tarragon

If you don't have tarragon, chop up some of the fennel fronds and toss them in.

Dice a bulb of fennel and a shallot or red onion. In a bowl, mix together about half a cup of plain yogurt, the fennel, the shallot, a drained can of tuna packed in oil, a teaspoon of chopped fresh tarragon, salt, and pepper. Serve in pita pockets, or rolled in large romaine lettuce leaves, with lemon wedges on the side.

25.

White Bean Toasts

Think of this as the Italian version of hummus.

Drain a can of cannellini or other white beans (or cook them yourself), reserving the liquid. In a food processor, puree the beans, some olive oil, a couple of teaspoons of fresh rosemary, fresh lemon juice, salt, and pepper; process until smooth, adding the reserved bean liquid as needed for consistency. Chop a handful of dried tomatoes (they can be dried or reconstituted) into thin strips. Spread the bean mixture on toasted peasant bread, top with a few bits of the tomatoes, and serve.

26.

Kale and Prosciutto Sandwich

*This sandwich gets even better topped with a few slices
of roasted red peppers or softened dried tomatoes.*

Roll four leaves of kale and slice them into half-inch ribbons. Cook in olive oil until wilted and softened; season with fresh lemon juice, salt, and pepper. Toast slices of sourdough or other good-quality bread; spread the toasts with goat cheese and a heaping spoonful of the kale; top with a slice of prosciutto.

27.

Panini with Mushrooms and Fontina

If you can make grilled cheese, you can make panini; just use another pan or lid to press on the sandwich while it cooks in a skillet.

Cook about two cups of sliced mushrooms in butter; season with fresh oregano or thyme, salt, and pepper. When the mushrooms have released their liquid and dried out, divide the vegetable mixture among slices of good-quality whole grain bread with thinly sliced fontina or other semi-hard cheese on top; add another slice of bread on top and brush the outside of both sides with olive oil or softened butter if you like. Cook the sandwich in whatever press you have until the bread is toasted and the cheese is melted, adjusting the heat as needed.

28.

Gruyère Apple Grilled Cheese

Add a couple bacon slices for smokiness (and, of course, meatiness!).

Butter slices of good-quality sourdough bread. Layer Gruyère cheese and thinly sliced tart apples and top with another slice of the buttered bread. Cook the sandwiches in a few tablespoons of melted butter—you can use a press or an ordinary skillet with a bit of weight on top of the sandwich—turning once, until the cheese has melted and the bread is golden brown on both sides, about eight minutes total.

29.

Figs in a Blanket

The name says it all.

Heat the broiler (you can grill these too). In a small pot, bring a cup of red wine, a few tablespoons of honey, a cinnamon stick, and a rosemary sprig to a boil. Wrap half of a fresh fig in half a slice of bacon. Arrange the figs on an oven-safe pan and broil for several minutes per side, until well browned. Serve with the reduced sauce.

30.

Turkey and Pear Wrap
with Curried Aioli

Leftover homemade turkey is ideal, but good-quality deli turkey is fine.

Mix half a cup of mayonnaise (or plain yogurt) with some minced garlic and about a teaspoon of curry powder. Lightly toast flour tortillas in a skillet for about 20 seconds per side. Spread the aioli on the tortillas; evenly layer a lettuce leaf, a thin slice of red onion, thinly sliced pears, and some turkey on top. Roll the tortillas tightly, cut them on the bias, and serve.

31.

Eggplant, Kalamata, Goat Cheese,
and Dried Tomato Sandwich

You can sear the eggplant in olive oil if you like.

Heat the broiler or a grill. Slice an eggplant into one-inch rounds and lightly brush both sides of the rounds with olive oil and sprinkle with salt. Broil or grill for two or three minutes per side, or until golden and softening in the center. In a food processor or blender, puree about a cup of pitted Kalamata olives, some dried tomatoes, and a couple of tablespoons of olive oil to form a paste. Spread goat cheese on ciabatta or other bread; top with a smear of the olive paste and a slice of eggplant.

32.

Seared Cauliflower with Olives and Breadcrumbs

To make this more substantial, start the recipe by frying a sausage or two (or a couple of chunked chicken thighs) in the pan first; break the meat into chunks as it cooks.

Core and roughly chop a head of cauliflower. Heat a film of olive oil in a large skillet over high heat and cook the cauliflower undisturbed, until it browns a little and begins to soften. Add a tablespoon of minced garlic and a handful of pitted olives; cook and stir for a couple of minutes, until the dish comes together and gets fragrant, adding a few more drops of oil to the pan as needed. Add fresh breadcrumbs and keep stirring until they're toasted. Taste and sprinkle with salt if needed, lots of black pepper, and some chopped parsley. Serve hot or at room temperature with lemon wedges.

33.

Broiled Brussels Sprouts with Hazelnuts

For something meatier, fry up a couple of slices of bacon or some diced pancetta and add it along with the hazelnuts.

Heat the broiler. Trim about a pound of Brussels sprouts and pulse in a food processor—or use a knife—to chop them up a bit. Spread out on a rimmed baking sheet, drizzle with two tablespoons olive oil, sprinkle with salt and pepper, and toss. Broil the sprouts for about five minutes, until browning on the edges. Meanwhile, pulse a handful of hazelnuts (or chop them). Shake the pan to flip the sprouts; add the nuts and broil for another three minutes. Sprinkle with freshly squeezed lemon juice and plenty of fresh parsley.

34.

Flatbread Pizza
with Figs, Goat Cheese, and Balsamic

Ripe figs make all the difference here, as does good balsamic vinegar.

Slice a couple of handfuls of figs into quarters. Brush olive oil on lavash or other flatbread and dot generously with goat cheese; spread the figs evenly on top of the cheese. Bake in a 450°F oven until the cheese melts and the figs soften. Drizzle with a tiny bit of balsamic and serve.

35.

Root Vegetable Stir-fry

For a more substantial meal, add strips of cooked chicken when you add the spices.

Use a food processor or box grater to shred a pound or so of one or more root vegetables: waxy potatoes, sweet potatoes, celery root, rutabaga, alone or in combination. Squeeze the shreds dry with your hands. Put a thin layer of vegetable oil in a large skillet over medium-high heat. When it's super hot, add a layer of the vegetables and sprinkle with salt and pepper. Stir-fry without stirring too much so that the shreds brown a bit and clump together. When the vegetables are just tender, season with curry or five-spice powder; stir a couple of times, remove to a serving plate, and repeat in batches with the remaining vegetables. Garnish with chopped cilantro or scallions and serve.

36.

Spiced Vegetables with Raisins

*To make this a little more festive, serve on a bed of couscous topped
with fresh mint and chopped pistachios.*

In a couple tablespoons of olive oil, cook a sliced zucchini; a carrot (chopped into one-inch rounds); a couple garlic cloves, lightly crushed; a teaspoon each of cumin and ginger; half a teaspoon cinnamon; and some salt. Cook for about three minutes. Add a small can of tomato paste and a half cup or so of water, and stir until blended. Add two cups of precooked chickpeas (canned are fine), a handful or two of raisins, the juice of a lemon, and a little more water if necessary; cover and bring to a boil. Reduce to a simmer and cook until the carrot is tender, about five minutes; then adjust the seasoning and serve.

37.

Butter Beans with Prosciutto and Mushrooms

Grate fresh Parmesan over this before serving if you like.

Cut a few slices of prosciutto into pieces about an inch wide, then cook it in a little olive oil until just crisp, about two minutes; remove and set aside. Add a cup or so of sliced mushrooms and drained precooked or canned (or frozen) butter beans to the pan. (There should be some fat left in the pan from the prosciutto; if not, add more olive oil.) Cook until the mushrooms soften a bit, three to five minutes. Add a quarter cup of white wine and continue cooking until the liquid reduces slightly. Sprinkle the vegetables with salt and pepper and serve, topped with the prosciutto.

38.

Stir-fried Mixed Vegetables with Ginger

Replace the broccoli with cauliflower, broccoli rabe, broccolini, or even celery.

Cut broccoli into florets and bok choy into strips. Blanch the broccoli in salted boiling water until crisp-tender; shock in ice water to stop the cooking; drain. Heat two tablespoons of sesame oil in a big skillet; add a tablespoon of freshly grated ginger and some minced garlic and stir; add a few chopped scallions, a diced fresh red chile, a few tablespoons of oyster sauce, a pinch of sugar, and the juice of a lime. Stir to combine well; add the broccoli florets and bok choy strips. Cook until the sauce is reduced slightly and coats the vegetables; add a bit of soy sauce, season with salt and pepper if necessary, and serve over noodles or rice.

39.

Garlicky Rabe with Pancetta and Pine Nuts

Adding more garlic is perfectly acceptable; the same goes for the chile flakes;
and of course you can follow these directions for almost any vegetable.

Chop about a quarter pound of pancetta into small pieces and cook in a bit of olive oil until just turning brown, about three minutes. Add some minced garlic and a pinch or two of red chile flakes; continue cooking for another minute or two until the garlic is soft and fragrant. Roughly chop a bunch of rabe and add it to the pancetta: raise the heat a bit and add a splash of water to make some steam. Continue cooking, stirring and adding more water or oil as needed until the rabe is heated and crisp-tender. Adjust the seasonings, toss with toasted pine nuts, and serve.

40.

Fried Endive with Butter and Lemon Sauce

An elegant side dish for almost any fish or meat.

Trim endive heads and halve lengthwise. Cook them in boiling salted water with a squeeze of lemon added for about three minutes. Drain and dip the pieces in milk, then in flour seasoned with salt and pepper. Cook in a few tablespoons of olive oil over medium-high heat for about two minutes per side; set aside. Add a few tablespoons of butter to the pan and continue cooking until it starts to brown, about 30 seconds. Add freshly squeezed lemon juice to taste and chopped parsley; let the sauce continue cooking to thicken a bit. Serve the sauce drizzled over the endive.

41.

Eggplant Stir-fry

Hoisin sauce (think of it as Chinese ketchup) is the main condiment for Peking duck and mu shu pork; it also makes a great dipping sauce for spring rolls.

Dice a medium-size eggplant into one-inch pieces and slice bok choy into strips. Cut firm tofu into one-inch cubes. Cook a teaspoon or so of grated ginger and minced garlic in sesame oil for about two minutes; remove. Add the eggplant and tofu to the pan and continue to cook until both begin to brown (work in batches if the pan is too crowded and add more oil as needed). Add the bok choy and the garlic and ginger, along with a few tablespoons of hoisin sauce and a little water; stir, then cook until the bok choy is wilted. Top with chopped scallions and serve with rice.

42.

Northern Beans with Spanish Chorizo

You can use any cooked sausage you like here, but chorizo is special.

Cut chorizo (Spanish smoked, not Mexican raw) into quarter-inch pieces and sear until slightly browned. Mix together some drained precooked or canned great northern beans or other white beans, a couple of tablespoons of olive oil, and a handful of chopped parsley. Add the chorizo and serve with crusty bread and a mound of arugula.

43.

Crisp Tofu 'n' Bok Choy

They'll take a few minutes longer to cook, but eggplant, broccoli,
or green beans can all be substituted for the bok choy, with great results.

Cut firm tofu into thin slices. Shallow-fry the tofu in oil until it browns on both sides. Drain on paper towels; pour off the excess oil (you want about two tablespoons left in the pan). Cook some minced garlic and a teaspoon or so of freshly grated ginger for about a minute before adding a few handfuls of sliced bok choy; continue cooking the bok choy until soft. Add the tofu to the pan to warm and serve over rice or noodles.

44.

Eggplant Rolls

These can be served with tomato sauce, but a drizzle of good balsamic is all they really need.

Heat a grill pan or skillet. Trim a large eggplant and cut into quarter-inch-thick slices *lengthwise*. Brush with olive oil and sprinkle with salt and pepper. Cook with olive oil over medium heat until golden brown and quite tender. Stir together about a cup of ricotta cheese and half a cup grated Parmesan cheese; add a handful of chopped fresh basil and some salt and pepper, and mix well. Spread a few tablespoons of the cheese mixture on each slice of eggplant, roll up, and serve.

45.

Braised Fish with Zucchini

Leave the skin on the fish if at all possible.

Season any sturdy fillets or steaks with salt and pepper. Slice a couple of zucchinis into disks; dice a couple of tomatoes (canned are fine). Heat a few tablespoons of oil in a skillet and cook the fillets, skin side down, until crisp, three minutes or a little longer; remove the fish. Add about a cup of white wine (or, even better, half white wine and half fish stock) to the pan along with the zucchinis and tomatoes and bring to a boil; reduce to a simmer and put the fish back in the pan on top of the vegetables, skin side up. Continue cooking until a thin-bladed knife pierces the fish with little resistance; put the fish in shallow bowls and stir some grated lemon zest and parsley into the sauce. Put the vegetables and broth in the bowls with the fish, drizzle with olive oil and a bit more salt and pepper, and serve.

46.

Walnut-Coated Fish

Pretty much any nuts—pecans, hazelnuts, peanuts,
and pistachios—can be used to make this type of crust.

Heat the oven to 400°F. Put about a cup of walnuts in a food processor and pulse a few times until the nuts are just ground, but not too fine. Add a small handful of parsley, a tablespoon or two of chopped thyme (or a teaspoon dried), salt, and a pinch of cayenne; pulse another once or twice to combine. Slice any sturdy fish fillets into large pieces and rub with olive oil, then press the walnut mixture on it to form a crust. Put in an ovenproof dish, drizzle with more olive oil, and cook, turning once, until golden brown and done in the middle, six to 12 minutes depending on their thickness. Serve on a bed of watercress with lemon wedges or vinaigrette.

47.

Baked Fish with Oregano, Lemon, and Olives

Very classic.

Heat the oven to 475°F. Score the skin of some fish fillets (any kind, really). In a mortar and pestle or small food processor, mix together a few cloves of garlic, salt, pepper, and a tablespoon or two of fresh marjoram or oregano; add some olive oil and lemon juice to make a paste. Smear the paste on the fish, covering it well. Bake the fish skin side up for about eight minutes, or until a thin-bladed knife pierces it with little resistance. Chop a handful of good-quality black olives and a little more herb and scatter them over the fish before serving.

48.

Salmon and Sweet Potato with Coconut Curry Sauce

Use a spicy curry powder or a pinch of cayenne if you want more heat.

Heat some vegetable oil and cook a thinly sliced onion and a minced clove of garlic for a couple of minutes until soft; add a tablespoon or so of curry powder and stir until fragrant. Add a can of coconut milk, a couple of diced sweet potatoes, a generous squeeze of lime juice, a few dashes of fish sauce if you like, and some minced fresh ginger; bring to a boil and simmer until the sweet potato is almost tender, about five minutes. Cut a couple of skinless salmon fillets into half-inch cubes and add them to the pan; reduce to a simmer and cook until the fish is just done, about five minutes more. Garnish with fresh chopped cilantro and serve over basmati rice.

49.

Seared Tuna with Capers and Tomatoes

Don't overcook the tuna, or it will become dry.

Sprinkle tuna steaks with salt and pepper, then sear in a very hot skillet or grill pan with a little olive oil, just a minute or so on each side. Add a couple of diced tomatoes (canned are fine), a few tablespoons of freshly squeezed lemon or lime juice, and a tablespoon or two of capers. Cover and reduce the heat to medium for about two minutes; you want to just warm the tomatoes while the tuna cooks a bit more. Serve the tomato-caper sauce spooned over the tuna.

50.

Stir-fried Shrimp with Chestnuts and Napa Cabbage

Frozen chestnuts work nicely in this dish.

Cook a tablespoon each of minced garlic and freshly grated ginger in a couple of tablespoons of hot vegetable oil until they sizzle; add a few handfuls of thinly sliced napa cabbage and cook, stirring, until it just starts to wilt. Add a cup or so of peeled cooked and chopped chestnuts and a handful of shrimp (chopped if they're large). Reduce the heat and continue cooking until the shrimp turn pink, about three minutes. Add two or three tablespoons of water, then soy sauce and sesame oil to taste; top with cilantro and serve.

51.

Pan-Seared Fish
with Spicy Lime Butter

Or try mixing the butter with chopped herbs, capers, anchovies,
or roasted garlic (alone or in combination).

Stir together about a half stick of softened butter, a finely chopped shallot, the zest of a lime and a good squeeze of its juice, a minced red chile, and a pinch or two of salt. Pat any type of fish fillets dry, season them with salt, and cook them quickly in a tablespoon each of olive oil and butter. Turn the fish once and cook until golden and cooked through, about five minutes. Serve the fillets with a generous spoonful of the compound butter on top.

52.

Seared Scallops with Almonds

"Dry" sea scallops are the best.

Sprinkle about a pound of scallops with salt and pepper. Heat a couple of tablespoons of butter until the foam subsides; add the scallops and cook for about two minutes on each side, until nicely browned but still quite rare; remove and set aside. Add a handful of chopped almonds to the same pan and cook, stirring, until the nuts brown. Add a half cup or so of dry white wine and cook over high heat until it's reduced to a syrup; add a bit more cold butter to thicken the sauce. Serve the sauce over the scallops, garnished with chopped parsley.

53.

Mussels in Tomato–White Bean Sauce

A handful of diced Spanish chorizo gives an extra boost if you want one.

Cook a clove or two of minced garlic in a couple of tablespoons of olive oil over low heat for about two minutes, or until fragrant. Add a large chopped tomato (a couple of canned ones are fine), two cups of drained precooked or canned white beans, and two to four pounds of cleaned mussels. Cook, covered, for about five minutes, or until all the mussels open (discard those that don't). Sprinkle the mussels with chopped parsley and serve with lemon wedges and good crusty bread.

54.

Sesame Shrimp Toasts

Better than any version you've had in a restaurant.

Heat the oven to 475°F. Slice a baguette in half lengthwise, put the halves face up on a baking sheet, and set them in the oven while it heats. Put shrimp in a food processor with some butter, scallions, soy sauce, a few drops of sesame oil, and a pinch each of sugar and salt. Pulse until the mixture forms a chunky paste. Smear the shrimp paste all over the bread and sprinkle with sesame seeds. Bake until the shrimp paste is pink and cooked through and the bread is crisp, about 10 minutes. Cool a bit, then cut up and serve with a salad.

55.
Braised Chicken with Olives and Raisins

Toasted pine nuts make a terrific garnish.

In a food processor, combine about a quarter cup of olive oil, a tablespoon of chopped fresh oregano, a handful of raisins, a handful of pitted green olives, a quarter cup of dry white wine, and a pinch or two of salt; pulse a couple of times—you want large pieces, not a paste. Sear chicken cutlets in a couple of tablespoons of olive oil, about two minutes on each side. Lower the heat, add the olive-raisin sauce, then cover and cook until the chicken is cooked through. Garnish with chopped parsley or toasted pine nuts.

56.
Stir-fried Chicken with Nuts

Cashews are my favorite, but peanuts or walnuts do just as well.

Put vegetable oil in a large skillet over high heat; when it's almost smoking, add about a pound of cut-up boneless chicken and sear without disturbing for about a minute; stir and cook for another minute. When the pieces are well browned, remove from the pan and pour in a little more oil if you need it. Add a sliced red bell pepper, a chopped onion, and some minced ginger or garlic and cook another few minutes, stirring only when necessary, until the vegetables wilt. Return the chicken to the pan, along with about a cup of halved cashews, a couple of tablespoons of water, and a few tablespoons of hoisin sauce. Continue cooking until the sauce bubbles and everything is well coated. Serve, sprinkled with a few chopped cashews or some chopped cilantro, or both.

57.

Lavender-Thyme Braised Chicken

*Rosemary is easier to find than lavender and works just as well,
but lavender is a nice change if you can find it.*

Season chicken cutlets with salt and pepper, then sear them in a couple of tablespoons of olive oil on both sides until brown, about four minutes total; set aside. Add a tablespoon more of olive oil or butter to the pan, along with some minced garlic, a tablespoon of crushed lavender flowers (or a tablespoon of finely minced fresh rosemary), and a teaspoon of fresh thyme; cook for about a minute. Add a half cup (or more) of Riesling and deglaze the pan. Add the chicken, cover, and continue cooking until it's done, another four minutes or so. Spoon the sauce over the chicken.

58.

Chicken with
Sweet-and-Sour Sherry Sauce

Also great with pork.

Heat the broiler. In a little olive oil, cook about a cup of roughly chopped shiitake or button mushrooms and about a quarter cup of chopped shallots until the mushrooms are browning on the edges. Add a couple of teaspoons each of honey and sherry vinegar and cook for about a minute, stirring to combine. Add about a quarter cup of dry sherry and a half cup of chicken stock and cook five more minutes, continuing to stir. Meanwhile, sprinkle quarter-inch-thick boneless, skinless chicken cutlets with salt and pepper, rub them in olive oil, and broil, turning once, until done, about six minutes. Spoon the sauce over the chicken and serve.

59.

Grilled Chicken
with Prosciutto and Figs

One of my favorite flavor combinations.

Heat a grill or grill pan. Pound chicken cutlets to a quarter-inch thickness; season with salt and pepper. Grill the chicken, turning once, for about five minutes or until cooked through. Slice a handful of fresh figs in half and grill them, flesh side down, until soft and warm. Put slices of prosciutto on the chicken cutlets to warm for a few seconds; serve with the grilled figs and a drizzle of good-quality balsamic.

60.

Chicken Curry in a Hurry

Add more curry if you like.

In about a tablespoon of oil, cook a sliced onion, teaspoon of curry powder and some salt and pepper for about three minutes. Season chicken tenders with salt, pepper, and more curry powder. Nestle the chicken between the onions, and cook for about two minutes on each side; remove the chicken and set aside. Add a cup of plain yogurt (or sour cream if you want it a bit richer) to the pan and stir, cooking for another minute or so (do not boil). Return the chicken to the pan and cook for another few minutes, turning once, until everything is cooked and warmed through. Adjust the seasonings and serve over couscous or jasmine rice.

61

Chicken Puttanesca

Cut chicken cutlets into half-inch pieces and toss them with salt and pepper. Chop six or more olive-oil-packed anchovies. Use a bit of the anchovy oil mixed with olive oil to cook the chicken and diced anchovies, cooking until the chicken turns white, about three minutes. Add a tablespoon of minced garlic, a can of crushed tomatoes, a handful of chopped black olives, a few tablespoons of capers, and a pinch of crushed red chile flakes. Cook until the sauce thickens and the chicken is cooked through, just a few minutes. Garnish with chopped parsley and serve.

62.

Sesame-Glazed Grilled Chicken

Serve with wilted bok choy or steamed broccoli.

Heat the grill or grill pan. Pound chicken breasts to a quarter-inch thickness. Mix together minced garlic, soy sauce, hoisin sauce, sesame oil, and cayenne to make a thin paste. Brush on the chicken and grill (or broil) until cooked through, turning once, about five minutes. Lightly toast sesame seeds in a dry pan until just starting to color. Sprinkle the chicken with the sesame seeds and garnish with chopped scallion.

63.

Chicken Teriyaki Skewers

Make this, too, with salmon, tuna, beef, or pork.

Cut a pound of chicken thighs or breasts into chunks; thread them on skewers. Combine four tablespoons of soy sauce, four tablespoons of mirin (or honey thinned with water), two tablespoons of sake, two tablespoons of sugar, and a few gratings of fresh ginger in a bowl. Put the skewers on the grill or under the broiler and baste them with the sauce every couple of minutes; continue cooking (and basting) until the meat is cooked through and a little blackened outside, about eight minutes total.

64.

Braised Pork with Rosemary

These chops won't dry out as long as you don't overcook them.

Rub boneless pork steaks or pork chops with olive oil, a clove or two of minced garlic, a tablespoon of fresh rosemary, and some salt and pepper. Sear in butter or oil until just brown on both sides; remove and deglaze the pan with a cup or so of dry white wine over high heat, being sure to scrape up all the brown bits left from the pork. Return the chops to the pan, along with any juices, reduce the heat, and cover. Continue cooking until the chops are barely pink inside, just a couple of minutes. Remove from the pan, turn up the heat, and reduce the liquid to a syrup; add a tablespoon or two of butter to thicken the sauce and adjust the seasonings. Serve the chops topped with the sauce and garnished with a little more rosemary.

65.

Fennel-Orange Braised Pork

The anise and citrus flavors in this preparation also work well with firm white fish.

Sprinkle boneless half-inch-thick pork chops with salt and pepper. Slice a bulb of fennel and an onion very thinly—a mandoline works well here—and break a peeled orange into segments. In some olive oil, sear the pork chops for about two minutes on each side; set aside. Add the fennel, onion, and orange to the pan and cook for a couple of minutes. Add a half cup of freshly squeezed orange juice and return the pork chops to the pan; cover and continue simmering for another six minutes or so, until the pork is cooked to desired doneness (add a little more juice, or some water or white wine, if necessary). Serve the pork with the sauce, fennel, onion, and orange slices; garnish with minced fennel fronds.

66.

Grilled Pork
with Shredded Brussels Sprouts

*Use a mandoline or slicing blade on a food processor
to make quick work of shredding the sprouts.*

Heat the grill or a grill pan. Rub boneless pork steaks with some minced garlic, salt, and pepper. Very thinly slice about two cups of Brussels sprouts. Heat a few tablespoons of butter, add the shredded sprouts, and cook until just wilted but still crisp-tender, about five minutes. Add a few tablespoons of freshly squeezed lemon juice, a tablespoon of poppy seeds, salt, and pepper. Meanwhile, grill the chops until brown on both sides but still a bit pink in the middle; serve on the sprouts.

67.

Sausage and Cabbage

Savoy or napa cabbage makes this a bit more delicate.

Cut some sausages into chunks and cook them in a large skillet with some olive oil over medium-high heat until crisp and almost done, five to seven minutes. Drain off any excess fat, then add some minced garlic and a small head of sliced cabbage to the pan along with a splash of red wine or water and a sprig of thyme if you have it. Cover and cook for about four minutes. Remove the lid and keep stirring and cooking until the cabbage is tender and the sausages are cooked through. Serve with baked potatoes or thick slices of whole grain toast and lots of mustard.

68.

Sausage with Red Lentils

Red lentils cook very quickly, so you'll want to keep an eye on them.

Slice a couple of sausages and cook them in a bit of olive oil until just beginning to brown; add a chopped onion, a chopped carrot, some minced garlic, and fresh thyme leaves. Cook a cup or so of lentils until done but not falling apart. Whisk together about a quarter cup of olive oil, a couple of tablespoons of red wine vinegar, a bit of Dijon mustard, salt, and pepper. Drain the lentils and add them to the sausage and vegetable mixture; toss with some of the vinaigrette, adding more as needed, and serve.

69.

Pork Tacos with Apple-Fennel Slaw

Pork from the shoulder is best here; and if you can't find fennel, use celery.

Heat a grill or grill pan. In a small bowl, combine a tablespoon each sugar, cumin, chili powder, and paprika, and a bit of salt; rub it into slices of pork. Slice a tart apple and a bulb of fennel (this is a great time to use a mandoline if you have one). Toss the apples and fennel with olive oil and lemon juice. Grill the pork, turning once, until browned and cooked; cut into strips and serve it in warm corn tortillas along with the slaw.

70.

West Indian Pork Kebabs

Fresh fruit salsa is the perfect side here; try chopped citrus, pineapple,
or mango mixed with some red onion, cilantro, chile, salt, and pepper.

Heat the broiler. In a bowl, combine some minced garlic, about a half teaspoon of ground allspice, a pinch of nutmeg, some fresh thyme leaves, a chopped small onion, and the juice of a lime. Toss this mixture with about a pound of pork shoulder cut into one-inch cubes. Thread the pork onto skewers and broil for about six minutes or until cooked through, turning to brown all sides evenly.

71.

Ham Steak with Redeye Gravy

A great way to use the morning's leftover coffee.

Sear a thick ham steak in a hot skillet with a fair amount of butter or olive oil. Remove the ham and use the fat to soften a sliced onion. Add some flour to the pan to coat the onion in a paste, and when the flour begins to turn golden, pour in a cup or so of coffee and stir until it thickens into a sauce. Return the ham to the pan to heat through, then serve the steak with some of the sauce and onion on top.

72.

Grilled Steak with Gorgonzola Sauce

Stilton, Roquefort, Maytag, or any good blue can fill in for Gorgonzola.

Heat the grill or a grill pan. Season a three-quarter-inch-thick steak with salt and pepper. In a small pan, heat a cup of white wine, a couple of handfuls of crumbled Gorgonzola, and a tiny pinch of nutmeg; cook until creamy and slightly reduced. Grill the steak, turning once, to the desired doneness. Serve the steak sliced and drizzled with the Gorgonzola sauce.

73.

Miso Burgers

Really more like mini meat loaves.

Mix about a pound and a half of ground beef (or pork) with a tablespoon of dark miso, a handful of panko, and some chopped scallions. Form several fat burgers and sear them on both sides in a little hot vegetable oil. When browned, add a splash each of sake and soy sauce to the pan, lower the heat, cover, and cook to desired doneness. Serve the burgers and pan sauce over rice or somen, with pickles on the side.

74.

Beef Paillards with Leeks and Capers

Grill the steak quickly and don't let it overcook.

Heat the grill or a grill pan. Cut beef tenderloin into four-ounce pieces and pound them to a quarter-inch thickness; season with salt and pepper. Slice several leeks into coins (be sure to rinse well) and toss with olive oil, lemon juice, and a spoonful of capers; partially cover and cook in the microwave until tender and juicy, just a couple of minutes. Grill the steaks over high heat (in batches if you need to) for a minute or less per side. Serve topped with the leek mixture.

75.

Beef Stir-fry with Ginger Noodles

I like rice vermicelli best here, but any thickness will work;
you'll have to boil them for a few minutes though.

Soak thin rice noodles in boiling water until soft, about 10 minutes; drain. In a tablespoon of sesame oil, cook about a tablespoon of grated ginger and a handful of chopped scallions for a couple of minutes, or until softened. Toss the ginger mixture with the noodles and set aside. In some vegetable oil, stir-fry thinly sliced beef for about two minutes; add a couple of handfuls of bean sprouts and cook for another two minutes. Add a little water and a little soy sauce and continue cooking until the sauce coats the beef and vegetables. Serve the beef and vegetables over the noodles.

76.

Lamb Chops
with Cranberry-Rosemary Reduction

The perfect accompaniment is wild rice,
but you'll need considerably more time if you go that route.

Combine a couple of cups of cranberries, a couple of tablespoons of brown sugar, a cinnamon stick, a sprig of fresh rosemary, and about a half cup of brandy in a saucepan and bring to a boil; continue cooking, stirring occasionally, until the mixture is reduced to syrupy consistency, about 10 minutes. Season lamb chops with salt and pepper; in a skillet with a couple of tablespoons of butter, cook the chops, turning once, for about eight minutes total (you want them well browned but still pink on the inside). Serve the lamb chops drizzled with the cranberry-rosemary sauce.

77.

Grilled Lamb Steak
and White Bean Mash

The bean mash is a perfect bed for the lovely lamb juices.

Heat the grill or broiler; season lamb steaks (from the shoulder preferably, or the leg) with salt and pepper. In a food processor, puree a can of cannellini beans (reserving the liquid) or precooked beans, a large clove of garlic, a tablespoon or two of fresh rosemary, a few tablespoons of olive oil, and freshly squeezed lemon juice to taste. Add a few tablespoons of the reserved bean liquid as needed (half-and-half, cream, stock, oil, or water will all work, too) to get a nice smooth consistency. Season the bean mash with salt and (lots of) pepper and add more lemon juice if needed. Grill or broil the steaks until done (medium or so is best). Slice the steaks and serve alongside the white bean mash.

78.

Braised Lamb Chops with Prunes

Serve with good crusty bread.

Chop a handful of prunes (if they're really tough, soak them in water for a few minutes first). Rub not-too-thin lamb chops with a spice mixture of ground cinnamon, ginger, cloves, salt, and pepper; cook chops in olive oil, turning once, for just a couple of minutes. Add the prunes and a glass of port, red wine, stock, or water; cover and cook until just done. Remove the chops and reduce the liquid to a syrupy consistency. Serve the chops topped with the prunes and liquid.

79.

Moroccan Lamb Chops with Couscous

A lot of chopping, but not much cooking.

Heat the broiler. Season lamb chops with some oregano, cumin, salt, and pepper; put them in one half of a shallow roasting pan. In a bowl, toss together a couple of tablespoons of olive oil, a few smashed cloves of garlic, a couple of handfuls of cherry tomatoes, a small eggplant, cubed, a sliced zucchini, salt, and pepper. When mixed, put the vegetables in the other side of the roasting pan. Broil the lamb and vegetables for about eight minutes; turn the lamb once and toss the vegetables so they brown on all sides. Serve the vegetables on a bed of couscous along with the lamb.

80.

Pasta with Balsamic Onions

This would be a cliché if it weren't so damn good.

Boil salted water for pasta and cook it; meanwhile, in a tablespoon or so of olive oil, sear a couple of sliced onions until nicely browned, stirring almost all the time. Splash some balsamic vinegar over all and sprinkle with salt and lots of black pepper; reduce the heat so the mixture thickens into a sauce. Drain the pasta, reserving some of the cooking water; toss the pasta with the onion sauce, adding some of the reserved cooking water as needed to moisten and serve; Parmesan cheese is optional.

81.

Pasta with Herbed Ricotta and Dried Cherries

For some crunch, garnish with finely chopped hazelnuts.

Boil salted water for pasta and cook it; meanwhile, chop a handful of fresh parsley, some oregano, and a few sage leaves. Mix the herbs with a cup of fresh ricotta and about a half cup of freshly grated Parmesan cheese; season with salt and pepper. In a tablespoon or two of butter over low heat, cook a couple of handfuls of dried cherries and a splash of red wine until the cherries soften a bit, about three minutes. Drain the pasta, reserving some of the cooking water. Add the pasta to the cherry mixture and stir to coat, adding some of the reserved cooking water to make a sauce; taste and season with salt and pepper. Serve the pasta with a dollop of the herbed ricotta on top.

82.

Mushroom Pasta

Some reconstituted porcini added to the fresh mushrooms give this a terrific earthiness.

Boil salted water for pasta and cook it; meanwhile, slice about two cups of fresh mushrooms and cook them in a couple of tablespoons of olive oil with some salt and pepper. When they're dry, add about half a cup of white wine and some minced garlic; cook until the wine reduces and the garlic mellows. Drain the pasta, reserving some of the cooking water. Toss the pasta with the mushrooms along with a handful of freshly chopped parsley; add cooking water if needed to moisten the sauce. Serve with lots of freshly ground pepper and grated Parmesan cheese.

83.

Cheesy Corn Bread Dumplings

Enrich the cooking liquid with leftover chicken, beans, or cut-up vegetables.

Bring a deep skillet of salted water or chicken stock to a boil. Mix together a cup each of flour and cornmeal, with a teaspoon of baking powder and a pinch each of baking soda and salt. Beat an egg with a little buttermilk and a couple of handfuls of grated cheddar. Stir the wet mixture into the dry, adding a little more buttermilk or flour as needed to create a stiff biscuit-like batter. With the help of a rubber spatula, drop large spoonfuls of the mixture into the liquid; bring to a steady simmer; cover and cook until set and a toothpick comes out clean, about 10 minutes. Fish the dumplings out with a slotted spoon and serve, garnished with chopped parsley and some of the stock if you used it.

84.

Penne with Vodka Sauce

A contemporary classic.

Boil salted water for pasta and undercook it slightly; meanwhile, use a big skillet coated with olive oil to cook some minced garlic, a pinch or two of red chile flakes, and a pinch of salt until the garlic is soft and fragrant. Add a can of tomatoes (that you've crushed or chopped a bit) and simmer for about five minutes, then add about a quarter cup each of vodka and cream. Drain the pasta and add it to the pan; toss the pasta well and give it a minute or so to absorb the sauce. Season with salt and pepper and garnish with chopped parsley.

85.

Pasta with Spinach, Currants, and Pine Nuts

Use raisins if you must; and cut pasta (like farfalle or fusilli) really works best here.

Boil salted water for pasta and cook it; meanwhile, toast a couple of handfuls of pine nuts in a dry pan until just fragrant and golden; set aside. In a few tablespoons of olive oil, cook a bunch of chopped spinach until wilted; season with salt and pepper. Add two handfuls of currants and continue to cook until warmed through. Drain the pasta (reserving some of the cooking water) and toss it with some olive oil and the spinach mixture, using enough of the water to moisten everything. Garnish with the toasted pine nuts and serve.

86.

Spicy Pork with Soba Noodles

Soba noodles cook in less than five minutes.

Boil salted water for the noodles and cook them; meanwhile, cut boneless pork into thin strips; toss with salt, pepper, and five-spice powder. In a couple of tablespoons of vegetable oil, stir-fry the pork until it's cooked through, about three minutes. Add a bit more oil and a couple of tablespoons each of soy sauce and rice wine vinegar; cook for 30 seconds more. Drain the noodles and put in a bowl. Top with the pork, a handful of thinly sliced scallions, a handful of chopped cilantro, and a few sliced daikon radishes; season with salt and pepper and serve.

87.

Pasta with Fried Eggs

Add crumbled bacon, some fried pancetta,
or a cup of breadcrumbs toasted in olive oil for a bit of crunch.

Boil salted water for pasta and cook it; meanwhile, fry four eggs in butter, keeping them very runny. Drain the pasta, reserving some of the cooking water, and toss it with a few tablespoons of olive oil or butter, lots of freshly grated Parmesan cheese, salt, pepper, and enough of the reserved water to moisten; top with the fried eggs. Roughly cut the eggs up and toss the pasta again to serve.

88.

Pasta Gratinée

Mac-n-cheese, only more substantial.

Heat the broiler. Bring small cubes of waxy potatoes and a couple of cloves of garlic to a boil in a big pot of salted water; when the water boils, add a pound of cut pasta (like penne or rigatoni). Cook for about four minutes, then add some chopped cabbage. In a couple of minutes more, the pasta should be al dente and the potatoes tender. Drain and drizzle some olive oil over everything, season it with salt and pepper, and toss a couple of times. Transfer the mixture to a shallow ovenproof pan or dish, sprinkle grated Parmesan cheese and breadcrumbs on top, broil until bubbly, and serve with a big salad.

89.

Zucchini and Garlic Fusilli with Pistachios

Equally delicious is a combination of zucchini and yellow summer squash.

Boil salted water for the fusilli and cook it; meanwhile, slice two zucchinis into thin disks. Toast a handful of pistachios in a dry pan until just fragrant and turning golden; set aside. Cook some minced garlic in a couple of tablespoons of olive oil until fragrant, add the zucchini slices and two tablespoons of water, season with salt and pepper, and cook until soft. Drain the pasta, reserving the cooking water. Toss the zucchini and garlic mixture with the pasta, adding more olive oil and water if needed; add the toasted nuts and serve with grated Parmesan cheese and plenty of freshly ground pepper.

90.

Apple Cider and White Wine Slushy

Use any sweet white or sparkling wine you like.

In a blender or food processor, combine a cup of apple cider, a half cup of Riesling, and about a quarter cup of sugar. Add ice and pulse; continue adding ice and processing until the desired thickness is reached (about three cups total). Serve immediately with a sprinkle of nutmeg or a cinnamon stick or an orange slice if you like.

91.

Caramelized Pears with Mascarpone

If you have the time, let the pears cook longer to soften and darken more.

Slice a couple of pears into eight pieces each and toss with a few tablespoons of brown sugar. In a couple of tablespoons of butter, cook the pears, along with a handful of pecans, until they're glossy on all sides, about four minutes. Whip together a half cup of mascarpone, a quarter cup of heavy cream, a tablespoon or two of brandy, and a tablespoon of sugar, until thick. Sprinkle the warm pears and pecans with a bit of allspice and serve them over the cream mixture.

92.

Pumpkin Crème Brûlee

It's not a custard, but it's good and serves a crowd of six to eight.

Turn on the broiler and put the rack about four inches from the heat. With an electric mixer or whisk, beat together a small can of pumpkin, eight ounces mascarpone, and a quarter cup of brown sugar; add a half teaspoon each of ground cinammon and ginger and a pinch each of allspice and salt. Spread evenly into an ovenproof baking dish or ramekins and sprinkle the top with a think layer of brown sugar. Broil for a few minutes, until the sugar melts, forming a crust. Serve immediately.

93.

Dark Chocolate Raspberry Pudding

As decadent as a fast dessert can be.

In a pan, heat two cups of cream with one-quarter cup of chopped dark chocolate. When the chocolate melts, about four minutes, add two tablespoons of cornstarch, two tablespoons of sugar, and pinch of salt. Stir until thickened, about four more minutes. Add a cup or more of fresh raspberries and mix to combine. Fill ramekins or pudding bowls with the chocolate mixture. Serve warm, topped with a few more raspberries and sliced almonds.

94.

Quick Lemon
Upside-Down Cheesecake

The same flavors as a creamy cheesecake, but without the structure; serve in bowls.

Combine one cup each of softened cream cheese and ricotta with a teaspoon of vanilla, the zest of a lemon and its juice, and sugar or honey to taste; mix until evenly blended and smooth. Put the cream cheese mixture into a glass pie dish. In a food processor, combine one sleeve of graham crackers and a cup of walnuts; pulse until crushed and somewhat even. Top the cream cheese mixture with the crushed graham crackers and walnuts, chill if you have time, and serve.

95.

Pound Cake with Mascarpone and
Marmalade

Also good with strawberry-rhubarb compote.

Spread mascarpone on slices of your favorite bakery pound cake and drizzle with warmed marmalade or honey.

96.

Chocolate Panini

You want excellent bread here, but not sourdough.

Sandwich bits or shavings of bittersweet chocolate between two thick slices of bread (like brioche, country-style French or Italian, or a sturdy whole grain). Butter both sides and grill in a hot skillet, using another pan on top with a couple of cans in it to weigh the sandwich down. When toasted, flip and cook the other side the same way. Meanwhile, thin a little strawberry or apricot jam with brandy, rum, or water. Cut the sandwich in quarters and serve hot, with the jam sauce on the side for dipping.

97.

Dessert French Toast

Called torrijas *in Spain; the technique is slightly different from what you're used to.*

Heat about a half inch of olive oil in a large skillet until hot. Soak thick slices of good bread in a mixture of milk, sugar, and salt; then dip them in beaten eggs, let them drain a bit, and pan-fry until crisp on both sides in the hot oil. (Watch out—they will splatter a bit.) Serve with a sprinkle of cinnamon sugar, or drizzled with honey, syrup, fruit compote, or melted chocolate.

98.

Brown Sugar Apple in the Microwave

Pears work just as well.

Core four apples and stuff the centers with raisins, walnuts, brown sugar, and butter. Set upright in a microwave-safe dish, drizzle some port wine or brandy over each, partially cover and vent, and cook for about five minutes, rotating the apples as necessary and basting with the juices. Serve drizzled with their warm syrup and sprinkled with cinnamon.

99.

Apples à la Mode

Try sprinkling a little cinnamon over the hot apples.

Peel and core four apples and cut them into quarter-inch slices. In a few tablespoons of butter, cook the apples for about four minutes; add about a quarter cup of calvados and sprinkle with brown sugar. When the apples have softened and browned, turn up the heat and reduce the liquid to a syrup. Serve over vanilla ice cream.

100.

Caramel Fondue

Be careful with the sugar—it goes from amber to brown very quickly. And it's hot.

In a pan, heat a cup of sugar with two tablespoons of water; cook until the sugar dissolves, swirling the pan occasionally. When the sugar turns amber, add six tablespoons of butter and carefully whisk until the butter melts. Remove the pan from the heat, add a half cup of cream, and whisk until smooth. Put the sauce in a bowl and serve with slices of apples, pears, or bananas, or with whole dried fruit for dipping.

101.

Sweet Couscous with Dried Fruit

Especially nice made with whole wheat couscous.

Bring three cups of water to a boil. When it does, stir in two cups of couscous, a handful of dried cherries, a pat of butter, and a drizzle of honey. Cover, remove from the heat, and let steep for five minutes or so (a little more for whole wheat couscous). Add some chopped cashews, chocolate chunks, or grated coconut (or all three!); fluff with a fork and serve warm.

Winter

The darkest season is a great one

for cooking. It's true that unless you live in the South or Southwest you're going to have a hard time putting gorgeous fresh vegetables on the table, but it's equally true that the early darkness, combined with the warmth provided by the stove, makes this a time when preparing dinner seems most appealing.

These dishes necessarily rely on traditional long-keeping ingredients like legumes, grains, and eggs, with a higher dose of meat and fish than in other seasons, yet the recipes are, as a group, fresh, light, and contemporary.

1.

Egg in a Hole with 'Shrooms

Heat a couple of tablespoons of butter in a skillet and add a cup of sliced mushrooms along with some salt, pepper, and about a teaspoon of dried oregano. Cook until the mushrooms give up their liquid and begin to brown; remove and set aside. Use a biscuit cutter (or a glass, or the lid of a jar) to make three-inch holes in the center of pieces of thickly sliced white bread. Heat an additional tablespoon or two of butter (more butter is better here), add all of the bread pieces to the pan, and cook for a minute until golden. Flip the bread and crack an egg into the holes of each slice, then cook until the whites are just set. Use a wide spatula to remove the bread from the pan. Season with salt and pepper and serve alongside the mushrooms and the center circles for dipping.

2.

Pancetta and Spinach Frittata

Beat four eggs; add a handful of freshly grated Parmesan, salt, and pepper. Cut about a quarter pound of pancetta into small pieces and fry in a tablespoon of olive oil; add a couple of chopped shallots and continue cooking until the pancetta begins to brown and the shallots have softened. Add a bunch of chopped spinach and cook until wilted and beginning to dry. Pour in the egg mixture and cook slowly until the eggs just set. Run under the broiler to brown for a minute if necessary if the top remains runny; serve hot, warm, or at room temperature.

3.

Japanese Egg Crepes

Serve on rice or in soup.

Put four eggs, a teaspoon sugar, a tablespoon of soy sauce, and a little salt in a bowl; whisk briefly. Pour some peanut or vegetable oil into an eight-inch pan (nonstick or well seasoned) over medium heat. Swirl the oil around when it's hot, and add about an eighth of the egg mixture, swirling again so it covers the pan. Cook till the top is just setting up, then flip and cook for about 15 seconds more. Repeat to make more crepes. Stack the crepes, let cool, cut into strips or roll and slice, and serve at room temperature.

4.

Bacon, Eggs, and Grits

You can also use sausage meat, ham, or Mexican-style chorizo.

Cut a few strips of bacon into one-inch pieces and fry; set aside. Bring four cups of water and a teaspoon of salt to a boil; in a steady stream, add a cup of grits and continue stirring until the mixture begins to thicken, in a few minutes. Remove from the heat, add two beaten eggs (they'll cook in the heat of the grits), about a quarter cup of cream, and a few chopped scallions. Serve the grits topped with the bacon and some chopped parsley.

5.

Eggs 'n' Capers

Cook a small handful of thinly sliced onion in butter for about three minutes. Beat four eggs with some salt and pepper, then pour the eggs over the onion; scatter a couple of tablespoons of drained capers into the pan. Cook the eggs as you would an omelet or scramble until they're no longer runny and just set. Serve on top of toasted bread.

6.

Leek, Sun-Dried Tomato, and Goat Cheese Frittata

Cook the chopped whites of two leeks with a handful of dried tomatoes in two tablespoons of butter, until softened; do not brown. Whisk together four eggs and some salt and pepper and pour over the leeks. Sprinkle with a handful of crumbled goat cheese. Cover the pan and continue cooking until the eggs are set. Remove the pan from the heat and put it under the broiler to brown for a minute before serving.

7.

Peanut Soup

Leftover shredded chicken is terrific here.

In a food processor, combine half an onion, a couple garlic cloves, and a stalk of celery; pulse until a thick paste forms. Cook the paste in butter, stirring, for about three minutes. Add one-half cup of peanut butter (or more), one cup of heavy cream, and about four cups of stock; stir (you might have to whisk) to combine; bring to a gentle boil. Reduce to a simmer; season with salt, pepper, and a little cayenne. Serve, garnished with chopped peanuts and parsley or cilantro.

8.

Cauliflower Soup

You might substitute truffle oil for the olive oil here if you have it.

Cut a cauliflower into small florets, then boil them in salted water until tender, about five minutes. Drain, reserving the cooking water. Put the cauliflower into a blender with a bit of the cooking water and some cream or half-and-half and blend to a smooth puree; add sufficient stock to make six cups. Season with salt and pepper, drizzle with olive oil, and garnish with chopped chives.

9.

Chickpea Soup with Saffron and Almonds

Try adding some diced chorizo with the onions and garlic.

In a couple of tablespoons of olive oil, cook a thinly sliced small onion, some smashed garlic, about a half cup of slivered almonds, salt, pepper, and a pinch of saffron for about five minutes. Add a can of chickpeas (or your own cooked; either with their liquid) and four cups of chicken broth or water; use a potato masher or wooden spoon to break down some of the chickpeas. Cook and stir until warmed through and serve with a sprinkling of chopped parsley if you like.

10.

Mixed Vegetable Soup

Try adding a spoonful of pesto or just really good olive oil right before serving.

Put a film of olive oil in a large skillet over medium-high heat and add some chopped onion, some minced garlic, a few broccoli florets, a chopped carrot, and a chopped celery stalk; cook until everything begins to soften. Add a few tablespoons of tomato paste and cook, stirring almost constantly, for another minute or so. Add a couple of chopped tomatoes (canned are fine; use the liquid, too), about five cups of water or stock, and some freshly chopped oregano and thyme, with some salt and pepper; bring to a boil. Reduce to a simmer and add some fresh or frozen peas and a couple of cups of chopped greens, like chard or kale; continue cooking until the greens wilt. Serve with crusty bread.

11.

Zuppa di Pane (Bread Soup)

I sometimes add an egg or two at the end of cooking, giving them a couple of minutes to cook before adding the croutons.

Heat the oven to 450°F. Cut good-quality bread into large cubes; toss with olive oil, salt, and pepper; and toast on a cookie sheet until golden. Meanwhile, cook some chopped onion in olive oil for about two minutes. Add a can of drained pinto, red, or white beans; six cups of stock; and a sprig of fresh thyme. Continue cooking until warmed through. Add a couple handfuls of chopped spinach and the croutons; stir until the spinach is wilted; season with salt and pepper; and serve, topped with a few more croutons.

12.

White Bean Stew

Pancetta or bacon makes a nice alternative to ham; render the meat in the oil before adding the garlic.

Cook some minced garlic in a little oil over medium heat until fragrant. Add a can of chopped tomatoes with their juice, a cup or two of broth (bean cooking liquid is fine), a couple cups of precooked or canned cannellini or other white beans, a handful of chopped ham, and some salt and pepper; bring to a boil. Cook until hot, then add a couple handfuls of spinach, baby arugula, or other tender greens, and cook, stirring, until the greens wilt. Meanwhile, brush a few slices of baguette or other good bread with olive oil, rub with fresh garlic, and toast until golden. Serve the stew on the bread slices.

13.

Chickpea and Zucchini Tagine

To make a thicker stew that you can serve over couscous, just drain the tomatoes.

Cook chopped onion, a sliced zucchini, some ground cumin, a pinch of saffron, and some salt and pepper in olive oil. When the onion is soft, add a can of drained chickpeas (reserving the liquid), along with a large can of chopped-up tomatoes, with their juice. Bring to a gentle boil, then reduce to a simmer and heat through; serve with a spoonful of plain yogurt and freshly chopped cilantro.

14.

Black Bean Soup

Add any cooked meat as you're heating the soup, to make this heartier.

In a food processor, combine about two cups of precooked or canned black beans with some of their liquid, a teaspoon each of cumin and oregano, and salt and pepper to taste. Puree the beans until smooth, adding a bit of chicken stock (or more liquid) if necessary for a thinner consistency. Heat the mixture, adding a cup of whole beans and enough stock to come to about six cups. Serve garnished with a spoonful of plain yogurt or sour cream and freshly chopped cilantro.

15.

Mixed Bean Soup or Stew

In a couple tablespoons of olive oil, cook a diced onion, carrot, and celery stalk until the vegetables soften, then add about four cups of precooked or canned beans (navy beans, cannellini beans, black beans, pinto beans, black-eyed peas, kidney beans, or chickpeas) with some of their liquid, a couple cups of water or stock, two bay leaves, and a sprig of fresh thyme. Bring to a boil and cook until the flavors blend and the beans are warmed through; add more liquid to achieve the consistency you like. Season with salt and pepper, remove the bay leaves and thyme sprig, and serve.

16.

Lima Bean Stew

Use any tender green you like here; arugula, baby spinach, and dandelion are all perfect.

Cook a package of frozen lima beans in a cup of water with some salt, butter, and minced garlic. When the beans are tender, puree half of them with most of the cooking liquid in a food processor until smooth; add some cream, half-and-half, or chicken broth to thin. Return the pureed bean mixture to the pan with the whole beans and season with salt and pepper. Add a bunch of tender greens and continue cooking until the greens are wilted. Add more liquid if necessary and serve, with a drizzle of good-quality olive oil and crusty bread.

17.

Shrimp Bisque

Shrimp stock is ideal here; make it by simmering shrimp shells in water for 10 minutes or so, then strain.

Bring four cups of shrimp stock to a simmer. Soften a diced onion, a minced clove of garlic, and a bit of fresh thyme leaves in butter until softened. Add about a pound of shrimp and cook for another two minutes, stirring occasionally, until the shrimp begin to turn pink. Stir in a couple of tablespoons of tomato paste, then the stock. Add about a cup of cream, then thin as needed with stock or water; season with salt and pepper, and serve, garnished with chopped parsley.

18.

Quick Cassoulet

This version is far from strictly traditional, but it maintains the spirit of the original and takes less than 20 minutes.

Cook a chopped onion, a couple of diced carrots and celery stalks, and some minced garlic in olive oil for a couple of minutes. Add a sliced smoked sausage and cook for about three minutes more, then add two or three cups of precooked or canned (drained) cannellini or other white beans and a cup or two of chopped-up canned tomatoes, along with a bay leaf, a couple of sprigs of fresh thyme, salt, and pepper. Cover and simmer until everything is warmed through and the vegetables are tender. Toss fresh breadcrumbs with some olive oil, salt, and pepper and toast until golden; serve on top of the cassoulet.

19.

Mixed Bean Chili

You want chili con carne? Just add ground beef to the onion and garlic and cook through before adding the beans.

Cook a chopped onion and some minced garlic in a little olive oil, along with chili powder to taste, a tablespoon or so of cumin, a teaspoon of oregano, salt, and pepper. Add a cup or two each of drained precooked or canned kidney beans, garbanzo beans, and black beans; one or two cups of chopped tomatoes (canned are fine; include their liquid), and some frozen corn kernels if you like. Continue cooking until everything is warmed through; adjust seasonings and serve, topped with grated cheese if you like, and freshly chopped cilantro.

20.

Warm Beet and Goat Cheese Salad

A handful of toasted walnuts makes this even nicer.

Put a few beets in a microwave dish, cover, and cook until just fork-tender (about five minutes). Run under cool water and slip the skins off, then cut into wedges. Mix some crumbled goat cheese with the juice of a lemon, a handful of chopped fresh dill (or a pinch of dried), a couple tablespoons of olive oil, a half cup of plain yogurt, salt, and pepper to taste. Dollop the dressing over the beets and sprinkle with chopped celery (and the celery leaves if you have them), some salt, and lemon zest; serve with toasted pita or good crusty bread.

21.

Seared Scallops with Romaine

Try watercress instead of romaine if you can find it.

Season scallops with salt and pepper, then sear the scallops for a few minutes in butter, turning once, until just browned on both sides. Drizzle a bunch of romaine lettuce with some olive oil, freshly squeezed lemon juice, salt, and pepper. Sprinkle the scallops with a bit more freshly squeezed lemon juice (some zest is nice here too) and some chopped parsley, and serve over the dressed lettuce with the pan juices.

22.

Date, Bacon, and Bean Salad

Arugula or watercress works best here, but endive, escarole, frisée, and so on, are all good.

Cut some bacon into one-inch pieces and fry until browned; drain off most of the fat. Add a can of drained cannellini beans to the bacon along with a handful or more of chopped pitted dates; continue cooking until everything is just warm. Serve over a big bed of bitter greens with good-quality whole grain bread.

23.

Scallop and Citrus Salad

Whisk together about a quarter cup of olive oil, a couple of tablespoons of freshly squeezed orange juice, a dash of balsamic vinegar, salt, and pepper; set aside. Peel a couple of small oranges and separate them into segments. Slice some grape tomatoes in half and dice a small red onion. Toss about a pound of bay scallops with some salt and pepper. Sear the scallops and onion in two tablespoons of butter until no longer translucent and just browning, about three minutes; squeeze orange juice over all. Combine the orange segments and tomatoes with mixed greens and toss with the dressing; serve the scallops and onion with their juices on top of the salad.

24.

Raw Beet Salad

Peel four or five medium beets and a couple of shallots; combine them in a food processor, pulsing until shredded but not pureed. Toss with olive oil, sherry vinegar, Dijon mustard, salt, and pepper. Add minced parsley, chives, tarragon, or dill and serve on top of greens or with toasted pita triangles.

25.

Warm Cabbage Salad with Bacon

You can serve this over greens, like arugula, or not;
I sometimes add a couple handfuls of homemade croutons to this.

Chop a few slices of bacon and cook until brown. Meanwhile, use a food processor to shred a small head of red cabbage and a red onion. Add them to the bacon and cook, stirring occasionally, until the vegetables are wilting. Add a tablespoon of mustard seeds, two tablespoons of sugar, and a quarter cup of red wine vinegar; continue cooking until the cabbage is tender and the liquid has evaporated. Adjust the seasonings and serve.

26.

Avocado, Citrus, and Radicchio Salad

Peel an orange and separate it into segments. Slice an avocado or two; cut a head of radicchio into quarter-inch-thick segments. Arrange the orange, avocado, and radicchio slices on a plate; drizzle with olive oil and any mild vinegar, like rice or Champagne. Season with salt and pepper, garnish with freshly chopped mint, and serve.

27.

White Salad

You can add a handful or two of raisins for a bit of sweetness if you like.

Blanch cauliflower florets in salted, boiling water for about two minutes; drain and shock in ice water to stop the cooking. Chop a small head of napa cabbage and a couple of heads of endive; thinly slice a small white onion. Whisk together about a quarter cup of olive oil, a couple of tablespoons of white wine or sherry vinegar, a teaspoon of coarse mustard, salt, and pepper. Toss the cauliflower, cabbage, endive, and onion with the dressing and serve.

28.

Squid Salad
with Red Peppers and Cilantro

The best store-bought roasted red peppers are piquillos; use them if you can find them.

Slice squid into quarter-inch rings. Whisk together a cup of olive oil, a few tablespoons of lime juice, a minced fresh chile, some minced lemongrass or lime zest, salt, and pepper. Slice roasted red peppers into quarter-inch strips. In a few tablespoons of olive oil, stir-fry the squid until it just turns white, about two minutes; season with salt and pepper. To serve, toss the squid with a couple handfuls of cilantro, the red peppers, and the dressing.

29.

Spinach Salad with Feta and Nutmeg

*Try adding a handful of nuts, cherry tomatoes, diced cucumber, olives, raisins,
or any chopped dried fruit to this salad.*

Put a tablespoon or two of sherry vinegar and a handful of crumbled feta in a bowl. Use a fork to mash up the cheese a bit; add some pepper and a small grinding of nutmeg. Continue stirring while slowly adding about three tablespoons of olive oil. Add about a pound of well-washed and dried spinach to the dressing and toss well; season with salt if needed.

30.

Vietnamese Rice Noodle
Salad with Crab

*Cleaned crab of all kinds is available all year round; I like vermicelli-size rice noodles here,
but any thickness will do if you boil them for a few minutes.*

Soak the rice noodles in boiling water until soft, about 10 minutes; drain, rinse, drain, and set aside. Mix two parts rice vinegar with one part fish sauce, a little sugar, and some salt. Toss the noodles with a handful of chopped scallions, a shredded carrot, a handful of chopped cilantro, about a cup of crabmeat, and the dressing. Taste and adjust seasoning, garnish with chopped peanuts and a little more cilantro, and serve.

31.

Pear, Bacon, and Goat Cheese Sandwich

A winning combination.

Fry a few slices of bacon until crisp. Smear slices of good bread with goat cheese and layer with thinly sliced pears and the bacon. Drizzle with a little balsamic vinegar and serve.

32.

Chorizo and Manchego Panini

Sort of like a Cuban sandwich.

Smear slices of good-quality bread with Dijon mustard; top with slices of smoked chorizo, thinly sliced manchego cheese, and thinly sliced dill pickle. Toast the sandwich in a press, in a waffle iron, or in a heavy pan using another pan or lid to weight the sandwich down; serve when the cheese has melted.

33.

White Bean and Salmon Sandwich

Sockeye is the best canned salmon, and it's really quite good.

Combine a drained can of cannellini beans, a drained can of salmon, some minced garlic, some finely chopped fresh rosemary, a tablespoon or two of olive oil, a couple of tablespoons of capers, salt, and pepper. Using a fork to slightly mash the beans, combine well; warm slightly if you like, or don't bother. Serve on toasted bread or on top of torn greens.

34.

Beef Tartar Crostini

Please don't use store-bought ground beef for this.

Pulse about a pound of beef sirloin or tenderloin in food processor. Put in a bowl and toss with an egg, a teaspoon or more of dry mustard, a tablespoon or more of Dijon mustard, a tablespoon or more of Worcestershire, at least a few dashes of Tabasco sauce, a handful of chopped scallions, some capers, a couple of anchovy fillets (optional), a bit of minced garlic, and plenty of salt and pepper; mix until just combined. Serve on thin slices of toasted bread.

35.

Wild Mushroom Crostini

Use any kind of mushrooms you like here; a combination is best.

Slice a pile of mushrooms, and cook them in a few tablespoons of butter with some minced garlic, fresh thyme, salt, and pepper. Continue cooking until the mushrooms release their liquid, then add a splash of dry white wine. Cook a few minutes more or until all the liquid has evaporated and the mushrooms are beginning to brown. Stir in chopped parsley, taste and adjust seasoning, and spoon onto good-quality toasted bread.

36.

Cabbage and Kielbasa (or Salami, or Linguica, or . . .) Sandwich

Sear slices of kielbasa or other garlicky cooked or smoked sausage in a pan. Remove, then cook cabbage slices in the same pan, adding a little oil if necessary (or a splash of beer); season with salt and pepper. Build sandwiches with good-quality sourdough bread, Dijon mustard, and the kielbasa and cabbage.

37.

Meatball Sub

*You might add some mozzarella and put the sub in the broiler
to melt the cheese just before serving.*

In a bowl, combine about a pound of ground beef, an egg, and a handful each of breadcrumbs, Parmesan, and freshly chopped parsley or basil, along with some salt and pepper. Make small meatballs (a melon baller can be helpful). Sear in butter or oil until the meatballs are browned on all sides and cooked through; spread a thin layer of tomato paste on toasted hero rolls and add the meatballs, along with any juices.

38.

Chorizo and Egg Rollup

Some queso fresco or other cheese sprinkled on the egg mixture before rolling is nice.

Squeeze Mexican chorizo from its casing into a hot skillet and toss in some chopped red onion; cook, stirring occasionally, until the meat is done and beginning to crisp. Crack a couple of eggs on top, turn the heat down, and cover; cook for about three minutes, or until the eggs set. Meanwhile, warm large flour tortillas. Carefully scoop the eggs and some of the chorizo onto the tortillas along with a dash or two of Tabasco, salt, and pepper, and a spoonful of salsa if you like; fold in the short ends of the tortilla and roll lengthwise to serve.

39.

Fondue

Use cubes of good-quality bread and lots of freshly cut vegetables for dipping.

Combine about one cup of white wine with a crushed clove of garlic in a pan; bring to a boil and reduce to a simmer. Mix a tablespoon of cornstarch with two teaspoons of water and set aside. Add about two cups each of shredded Gruyère and Emmentaler cheese to the wine mixture, whisking until just melted. Add the cornstarch mixture and cook until creamy (do not boil); add more wine if needed for consistency. Serve, with the bread and vegetables (and if you don't have long forks, skewers!).

40.

Beer Batter Shrimp Po' Boy

As good as it sounds.

Heat oil for frying. In a bowl, mix together one can of beer, one and one-half cups cornmeal and pinches of salt, pepper, and paprika. Dip shrimp into the batter and fry in batches until golden, about three minutes. Serve on split crusty Italian or French loaves with lettuce, tomato, and mayonnaise; lemon juice and hot sauce are also great here.

41.

Prosciutto-Egg Sandwich

Hard-boil eggs; as they're cooking, sear slices of prosciutto in olive oil until crisp, just a couple of minutes. Shell the eggs, slice them, and mix with just enough mayonnaise to moisten, and a sprinkle of salt and pepper. Use the egg mixture to fill hard rolls or toasted brioche; top with the crumbled prosciutto, and finish with a few dashes of good olive (or truffle) oil.

42.

Braised Cabbage
with Spanish Chorizo and Beans

You can use linguica or kielbasa in place of chorizo, and any greens you like.

Slice smoked chorizo into quarter-inch-thick pieces, then cook in olive oil until it begins to crisp. Slice a head of green cabbage into eight wedges and put it on top of the chorizo; add a couple of cups of cooked or drained canned cannellini or other white beans, spreading to surround the cabbage; cover and cook for a few minutes, then flip the cabbage and stir the beans. Continue cooking until everything is warmed through, season with salt and pepper, and serve topped with toasted breadcrumbs or croutons and a drizzle of olive oil.

43.

Tofu with Pineapple and Red Peppers

Use precut pineapple, and this is even faster.

Chop half a pineapple and a large red pepper into half-inch pieces and cook for about three minutes in a bit of oil. Remove. Add more oil if necessary, followed by two cups of cubed firm tofu and a tablespoon each of minced garlic and ginger; cook and stir about three minutes more. Off heat, toss with a splash each of soy sauce and rice vinegar and some chopped scallions. Serve over rice.

44.

Mini Cannelloni

Heat the oven to 400°F. In a bowl, mix together a cup of ricotta cheese, a tablespoon of chopped sage, salt, pepper, and grated Parmesan. Put about a teaspoonful of this mixture in a wonton wrapper, roll into a tube, and put on a baking sheet lined with parchment paper. Brush or spray with olive oil. Bake for about 10 minutes, or until the wontons are crisp. If you don't have tomato sauce to warm up, serve drizzled with balsamic vinegar and sprinkled with lots of black pepper.

45.

Crisp Tofu and Asian Greens with Peanut Sauce

Use baby bok choy, Chinese broccoli, or tatsoi here; napa cabbage is a great alternative too.

Slice firm tofu into strips or cubes and pat dry; roughly chop a bunch of the greens. Pan-fry the tofu in some vegetable oil until it browns on all sides, about four minutes; remove and pour off all but a little of the oil. Add the greens and a pinch or two of red chile flakes, and continue cooking until the vegetables turn dark green, about three minutes. Mix together a half cup of peanut butter, a couple of tablespoons of soy sauce, and fresh lime juice to taste; add a bit of water if necessary to get a nice consistency. Add the sauce to the pan along with reserved tofu and toss to coat. Garnish with crushed peanuts and serve.

46.

Potato Cumin Curry

For more heat, add a freshly chopped chile along with the onions.

Peel and cut four baking potatoes into half-inch pieces. In oil, cook a thinly sliced onion until just soft, about two minutes; add a couple of tablespoons of curry powder, a tablespoon of cumin, and a pinch of saffron. Add the potatoes and toss to coat with the spices. Then add a can of coconut milk; fill the can with water and add that, too. Bring the mixture to a steady bubble; cover and cook until the potatoes are almost tender, about eight minutes. Add a drained can of chickpeas. Combine well and continue cooking until the potatoes are tender and the beans are warmed through. Serve topped with freshly chopped cilantro.

47.

Lettuce-Wrapped Fish

Any thick white fish fillets will work here.

Blanch large romaine or Bibb lettuce leaves in boiling water—one or two at a time—until tender and flexible, just a few seconds, and drain; then cut out the large central vein if necessary to roll. Put a piece of fish on each leaf and sprinkle with salt and pepper; fold or roll the fish in the leaves so the edges overlap. In a large pan or casserole with a cover, bring one cup of wine to a boil with two tablespoons of butter; reduce to a simmer and add the fish packages. Cover and cook until a knife easily penetrates fish, five to 10 minutes; remove the fish to a warm platter. Over high heat, reduce the liquid; when it thickens a bit, pour it over the fish and serve.

48.

Seared Fish with Cumin and Lemon

Any sturdy fish works here, including salmon, shrimp, scallops, or squid.

Combine about a half cup of flour with a tablespoon of cumin, and some salt and pepper. Lightly dredge the seafood in the cumin-flour mixture; cook the fish in a mixture of butter and oil until golden, turning once, about three minutes on each side. Sprinkle with freshly squeezed lemon juice and parsley, then serve with the pan juices.

49.

Shrimp with Black Bean Sauce

You can find fermented black beans at Asian markets and even most supermarkets.

Soak two or three tablespoons of black beans in about a quarter cup of sherry or white wine (or water in a pinch). Cook minced garlic in vegetable oil, along with a teaspoon of grated ginger and a pinch or two of red chile flakes. When fragrant, add about a pound of small shrimp and fry until just cooked through, about a minute. Add the black beans and their liquid, toss, and remove from the heat. Add a bit of soy sauce and toss again. Serve with jasmine or other rice.

50.

Mussels in White Wine and Garlic

Wild mussels are always more flavorful than farm-raised; wash them well, and discard any with cracked shells or those which don't close when you tap them.

Cook some minced garlic in olive oil for a couple of minutes; add a half cup of white wine and bring to a boil. Add two (or more) pounds of mussels to the pot, cover, and cook for five minutes, or until the mussels open (discard any that don't open). Serve the mussels in bowls with the broth, freshly chopped parsley, and slices of good baguette for soaking.

51.

Broiled Squid

Keep the cooking time very short, and your squid will stay tender.

Heat the broiler. Combine about a half cup of olive oil, a few tablespoons of sherry vinegar or freshly squeezed lemon juice, a tablespoon or so of freshly chopped rosemary, salt, and pepper; add a pound or two of cleaned squid and marinate for about five minutes. Remove the squid from the marinade and broil for about three minutes, shaking the pan once or twice, then serve with bread (toasted bread rubbed with garlic and drizzled with olive oil is quite fine here).

52.

Seafood Couscous

You can use almost any fish or shellfish you like here.

Add a bag of frozen peas, two cups of couscous, and a pinch of saffron to three cups of boiling water; stir, cover, and remove from the heat and let sit for about 10 minutes. Meanwhile, cook a chopped onion, a sliced red pepper, and some minced garlic in some olive oil for about two minutes. Add half a pound each of firm white fish and half a pound of fresh squid rings; stir-fry for about three minutes more. Fluff the couscous with a fork and serve the fish and vegetables over it; garnish with freshly chopped parsley leaves.

53.

Shrimp with Lemongrass

When you're mincing lemongrass, peel off its outer few layers to get to the tender inner core.

Cook a tablespoon of minced lemongrass in some vegetable oil; add minced garlic and a teaspoon or so of lime zest, then a pound or more of shrimp. Stir, then cook until the shrimp are no longer translucent, three to five minutes. Add some fish sauce to taste, then add some black pepper, and serve, sprinkled with cilantro.

54·
Scallop Stew with Couscous

A North African–flavored dish that you can spice up or down depending on your taste.

Cook couscous as in recipe 52, with or without peas and saffron. Soften a diced onion, some minced garlic, a teaspoon of cumin, a pinch of cayenne, half a teaspoon of cinnamon, and salt to taste in a couple of tablespoons of olive oil for about three minutes. Add a large drained can of chopped tomatoes and a handful of golden raisins; bring to a boil and simmer for five minutes. Add about a pound of scallops and continue cooking until they're opaque, three to six minutes depending on their size. Serve the stew over couscous with chopped cilantro on top.

55·
Citrus-Braised Fish
Fillets or Steaks

Try orange juice, lime juice, or any other combination of citrus juices here.

Sear sturdy fish fillets or steaks for about two minutes on each side in a little oil, until nicely browned. Add a quarter cup each of grapefruit juice and lemon juice, a tablespoon or two of soy sauce, some minced garlic, and about a teaspoon of freshly grated ginger. Cover and braise for about six minutes, or until the fish is cooked through. Serve over shredded red cabbage and sliced radishes.

56.

Simplest Chicken Kebabs

Lamb, beef, or firm fish all take to this preparation equally well.

Heat the broiler. Cut a pound of boneless, skinless chicken thighs into chunks slightly larger than one inch. Toss the meat with a minced onion, some minced garlic, a few tablespoons of lemon juice, olive oil, salt, pepper, a crumbled bay leaf, and about a teaspoon of oregano (fresh is best, but dried is OK; use less). Thread the chicken pieces on skewers and broil, turning occasionally, until browned and cooked through, about six to eight minutes. Serve with lemon wedges.

57.

Chicken in
Spicy Basil-Coconut Sauce

If you like more heat, don't seed one or both of the chiles.

Season chicken cutlets with half a teaspoon each of ground coriander, ground cinnamon, chili powder, and salt and sear them on both sides in a couple of tablespoons of olive oil. Remove from the pan, add more oil if needed, and cook sliced red onion, three minced cloves of garlic, and two seeded Thai chiles for about four minutes. Return the chicken to the pan along with about a cup of coconut milk, a couple dashes of fish sauce, and a few tablespoons of chopped basil. Cook until the coconut milk begins to bubble; reduce to a steady simmer and continue cooking until the chicken is done. Serve the chicken and sauce over rice with fresh lime wedges, garnished with more basil, or cilantro or mint (or all three).

58.

Chicken Paprikash

This can be served over couscous too, but if you have the time,
bulgur gives this stew a richer earthiness.

In two tablespoons of butter, sear a pound of boneless, skinless chicken pieces, about a minute on each side. Add a thinly sliced large onion, two crushed garlic cloves, a teaspoon of minced ginger (or half a teaspoon of ground ginger), three tablespoons of Hungarian paprika, a bay leaf, and a couple of teaspoons of salt; cook for about three minutes. Add a cup of chicken broth and bring everything to a boil. Reduce the heat and continue cooking until the chicken is just done; stir in half a cup of sour cream and serve over buttered egg noodles.

59.

Chicken Curry with Raisins

I like this topped with a handful or two of chopped peanuts and lots of fresh cilantro.

Cut boneless, skinless chicken breasts into one-inch pieces; sear them in hot vegetable oil until browned all over, just a couple of minutes. Remove from the pan, add more oil if needed, and soften a sliced red onion and a thinly sliced stalk of celery for about two minutes. Return the chicken to the pan along with two tablespoons of curry powder, a good pinch of salt, a cup of raisins, and a quarter cup of apple juice (or water); cover and continue cooking until the chicken is done, about three minutes.

60.

Chicken with Apples and Sage

Peel a couple of tart apples and slice them into pieces. Brown the chicken on both sides in some olive oil, about four minutes total; set aside. Add two tablespoons of butter, the apples, a diced shallot, and a tablespoon of brown sugar to the pan and cook for about three minutes. Add a cup of chicken broth, a tablespoon of cider vinegar, and freshly chopped sage, and stir to deglaze the pan and thicken a bit. Return the chicken to the broth and cook until the chicken is done, the apples are tender, and the sauce is reduced. Serve the chicken and apples with the sauce spooned on top.

61.

Coq au Vin

Classic French flavors.

Pound boneless, skinless chicken breasts (or thighs) to half-inch thickness and season with salt and pepper. Sear on both sides in a bit of butter; set aside. Add two carrots chopped into one-inch pieces and half an onion cut into wedges; cook until the onion begins to soften. Add a cup of red wine, a bay leaf, a teaspoon of fresh tarragon, and a thyme sprig; deglaze the pan, return the chicken to the pan, and cover. Simmer for about six minutes until the meat is cooked through and the vegetables are tender.

62.

Honey-Orange Chicken

Boneless pork chops are also terrific here.

Pound chicken breasts to half-inch thickness and season with salt and pepper. Mix together one-half cup of orange juice, one-half cup of honey, one tablespoon ground cumin, salt, and pepper. Sear the chicken on both sides in two tablespoons of vegetable oil for about four minutes total. Add the orange juice–honey mixture, cover, and allow it to simmer for about six minutes. Serve over mixed greens.

63.

Chicken Livers with Broad Noodles

Fettucine or—even better—pappardelle are what you want here.

Soften a chopped onion and a chopped celery stalk for about two minutes in a little olive oil. Add a half pound of ground meat—pork, beef, lamb, chicken, or turkey, whatever you like—plus four roughly chopped chicken livers and a few sprigs of thyme or sage leaves. Cook until the meat loses its redness, about six minutes. Add a couple of tablespoons of tomato paste along with some water and cook until everything is heated through. Serve over thick noodles sprinkled with freshly grated Parmesan cheese and parsley.

64.

Maple-Ginger Glazed Chicken with Pecans

A side of roasted Brussels sprouts really hits the spot here.

Combine a quarter cup of maple syrup with about a quarter cup of chopped pecans and a teaspoon freshly grated ginger in a bowl; mix to coat the pecans and set aside. Season half-inch-thick chicken cutlets with salt and pepper; sear the cutlets in a couple of tablespoons of butter, until browned, about four minutes total. Add some more butter to the pan and pour the syrup-pecan mixture over the top of the chicken, then cook the chicken for a couple of minutes more on each side, moving the chicken around the pan to coat it evenly. Serve the chicken topped with the warm pecans and the pan juice.

65.

Coconut-Orange Chicken

Nice with mixed greens and fresh orange wedges.

Brush half-inch-thick boneless, skinless chicken breasts with olive oil; season with salt and pepper and dredge lightly in flour. Cook a teaspoon of minced garlic, the minced zest of an orange, and a teaspoon of red chile flakes for about two minutes in olive oil; add the chicken and sear for about two minutes on each side. Add a can of coconut milk, a pinch of saffron, and a bay leaf; stir, cover, and let simmer for about six minutes until the chicken is cooked through. Sprinkle with slivered almonds and cilantro and serve.

66.

Chicken with Bacon, Shallots, and Brandy

Use thick-cut bacon here.

Cut a few slices of bacon into one-inch pieces and fry until crisp; remove with a slotted spoon. Season half-inch-thick chicken cutlets with salt and pepper and sear them in the bacon fat until browned, about two minutes on each side; remove and set aside. Add four sliced shallots and a teaspoon of minced garlic and cook for another two minutes; return the chicken to the pan, add a half cup of brandy, cover, and let simmer for about five minutes, or until the chicken is done and the sauce has thickened somewhat. Serve the chicken topped with the shallots, bacon, and sauce.

67.

Chicken Poached in Port

Pound chicken cutlets to half-inch thickness and season with salt and pepper. Cook a chopped onion in butter with salt and pepper for about two minutes. Add about a cup of port to the pan along with the chicken and a couple of bay leaves; bring it to a boil; reduce to a bubble, cover, and simmer for about four minutes. Spoon the onions and sauce over the chicken and sprinkle with freshly chopped parsley.

68.

Honey Fried Chicken

Freshly made breadcrumbs are best here; panko are also nice.

Combine half a cup of flour, about half a cup of fresh breadcrumbs, a tablespoon paprika, an egg, about half a cup of milk, salt, and pepper; mix until a thick batter forms (add a little more milk if necessary). Pound boneless, skinless chicken breasts to half-inch thickness and dip them in the batter until coated. Shallow- or deep-fry the breasts in oil until golden and cooked through, turning once, about eight minutes total. Warm some honey with some water and a sprig of thyme and drizzle it over the chicken to serve.

69.

Chicken Piccata

Boneless pork chops are also good prepared this way.

Dredge chicken breasts, pounded to half-inch thickness, in flour mixed with salt and pepper. Sear the chicken on both sides in a mixture of oil and butter, about four minutes total. Lay very thinly sliced lemon rounds on top of the chicken, add a cup of white wine, and cover; continue cooking for about five minutes. Remove the chicken from the pan and reduce the wine to a syrupy consistency. Serve the chicken with the lemon slices on top, a spoonful of the sauce, and a sprinkling of capers or chopped olives.

70.

Turkey Cutlets with Walnuts and Sage

*You might puree an apple or two in the food processor with a dash of cinnamon
to serve alongside the turkey.*

In a food processor, combine a handful or so of walnuts with about a half cup of breadcrumbs, a few tablespoons of freshly grated Parmesan cheese, a teaspoon or so of fresh sage, salt, and pepper. Pound turkey cutlets to half-inch thickness; season with salt and pepper; dredge in flour, egg, and the walnut mixture, pressing gently to help the mixture adhere. Heat a few tablespoons of olive oil and fry the cutlets, turning once, until golden and cooked through, about eight minutes.

71.

Sausage and Potatoes

Simply classic.

Heat the broiler. Slice potatoes into half-inch pieces and boil in salted water until soft, just a few minutes. Meanwhile, slice a few Italian sausages—sweet, spicy, or a combination—into two-inch pieces and put them in an oven-safe dish with half of a thinly sliced onion; broil until the sausage is well browned, about eight minutes, turning once. Mix the sausage, onion, and potatoes together in a bowl with a few tablespoons of olive oil and a handful of chopped basil or parsley.

72.

Sweet Sauerkraut with Kielbasa

*A chopped or pureed apple—or good-quality applesauce—can be used instead
of the pear.*

In some butter, sear three-inch pieces of kielbasa, a sliced onion, and a couple of chopped pears (slightly short of ripe is fine); cook for about four minutes. Add a bag or jar of sauerkraut (do not use canned), cover, and heat until warmed through, about six minutes more. Serve with pumpernickel rolls.

73.

Braised Pork Chops
with Celery Root

Use parsnips or carrots if you can't find the celery root.

Cut some celery root into half-inch sticks. Take thin, boneless pork chops and smear them with salt, pepper, and minced garlic. Sear in a mixture of butter and oil, turning once, about two minutes on each side; add the celery root and a splash of dry white wine and cover. Cook for about five minutes; remove the chops to a plate and cook until the celery root is just tender and the remaining liquid is reduced to a syrup. Add a bit of fresh butter and return the chops to the pan, along with any liquid that's accumulated around them. Turn once or twice in the sauce and serve, sprinkled with fresh parsley.

74.

Seared Pork Paillards with Prunes
and Olives

A surprising and good combination.

Pound boneless pork chops to quarter-inch thickness and sprinkle with salt, pepper, and some ground coriander. Sear the chops for about a minute per side in olive oil. Remove from the pan and add about a cup of white wine and a couple of tablespoons of butter; bring to a boil. Reduce to a simmer and add a handful of chopped prunes and a few chopped green olives; cover and cook for a couple of minutes, then add the pork and cook until just done, about three minutes more. Serve the pork drizzled with the sauce and garnished with chopped parsley or chives.

75.

Stuffed Pork Chops with Broccoli Rabe

A bit of a sprint, but worth the effort.

Remove a couple of sweet Italian sausages from their casings and brown in a bit of olive oil, breaking up the meat with a fork or spoon. Meanwhile, cook a bunch of chopped broccoli rabe in boiling, salted water until crisp-tender, about two minutes; drain. Pound boneless pork chops as thinly as you can; season with salt and pepper. Put a bit of the cooked sausage in the center of each of the chops, roll, and secure with toothpicks. Sear in the same skillet, browning the meat well. Drizzle the broccoli rabe with good-quality olive oil, sprinkle with salt and pepper, and serve with the stuffed pork chops.

76.

Steak au Poivre

The classic (and wonderfully excessive) recipe.

Salt and heavily—really heavily—pepper inch-thick steaks—rib eye, sirloin, or skirt (which will be thinner), and cook them in a grill pan to the desired doneness, turning once. Set the steaks aside. Melt some butter in the same pan with a couple of tablespoons of chopped shallot; cook until the shallot softens, about two minutes. Add a splash of brandy to the shallots, along with any collected juices from the steak, and reduce; lower the heat, add a bit of cream, and cook until it begins to thicken. Serve the cream sauce with the steaks.

77.

Beef Fajita Stir-fry

Some garnishes might include fresh cilantro, sour cream, guacamole, chopped tomato, or black olives.

Fry about a pound of thinly sliced sirloin steak in some olive oil over high heat until seared but still rare. Remove; add more oil if needed; add sliced red bell pepper, chopped onion, and garlic and stir-fry until just soft. Season with dried oregano, chili powder, salt, and pepper, and return the meat to the pan along with a couple handfuls of good tortilla chips and some crumbled queso fresco. Toss until the chips are well coated and serve with salsa drizzled on top.

78.

Scallion-Stuffed Beef Rolls

These are known as negima *in Japan, where they originated.*

Heat the broiler. Cut strips of flank steak into three-by-five-inch pieces about a quarter-inch thick. Brush one side of the beef with a little soy sauce. Cut scallions in half the long way, then into five-inch lengths; put two or three pieces on each piece of beef. Roll the beef lengthwise and secure with a toothpick or two. Broil as quickly as you can until browned, maybe five minutes total, turning halfway through. Serve, garnished with chopped scallions, cilantro, and a drizzle of soy and—if you like—sesame oil.

79.

Seared Calf's Liver with Celery

The nearly universal problem with liver is overcooking;
keep the cooking time short, and it will be delicious.

Heat two tablespoons of butter until the foam subsides; dredge a thick slice of liver in flour, shaking off the excess, and put it in the hot butter, sprinkling with salt and pepper. As soon as the liver browns on one side—two to three minutes—turn it and brown the other side, cooking for another two minutes. The liver should be medium-rare. Remove from the pan and add a couple of sliced celery stalks and the juice of a lemon or two. Stir to cook the celery a bit and make a little pan sauce. Serve over the liver, garnished with parsley or chives.

80.

Apricot-Braised Lamb Chops

Lovely over a bed of arugula or other spicy greens.

In a food processor, make a paste from a handful of dried apricots, some lemon juice, a bit of onion, a teaspoon of ground coriander, and a clove of garlic. Salt and pepper not-too-thin lamb chops and sear them in olive oil for about two minutes on each side until browned; remove and set aside. Add the apricot mixture to the pan along with a splash of white wine and bring to a simmer. Put the chops back in the pan, cover, and braise for about five minutes—they should remain pink inside. Serve, drizzled with the braising liquid.

81.

Red Wine–Braised Lamb Chops

Serve these over a bed of couscous tossed with peas.

Salt and pepper not-too-thin lamb chops and sear them in oil, turning once, until they're brown on both sides; set aside. Add a couple of tablespoons of flour to the pan, stirring constantly, until it's well combined with the drippings. Whisk in a half cup of beef broth or water, a half cup of red wine, some minced garlic, and a teaspoon or two of chopped fresh rosemary; bring to a boil. Return the chops and juices to the pan and cook, turning the lamb over once or twice until it's done.

82.

Indian-Style Lamb Kebabs

This preparation also works well with chicken, beef, and even firm fish.

Heat the broiler. Cut a pound or so of lamb shoulder into one-inch chunks. Toss with a cup of plain yogurt, a chopped small onion, some minced garlic, a teaspoon each of ground cumin, coriander, and paprika, and a pinch of cayenne. Thread the lamb pieces on skewers and broil, turning occasionally, until nicely browned and cooked to desired doneness. Serve with slices of fresh limes and freshly chopped cilantro or mint.

83.

Pasta Jambalaya

You can use any cooked sausage here, but the spiciness of andouille is the most authentic.

Boil salted water for pasta and cook it (use short-cut pasta like orzo, orecchiette, shells, or ditalini). Meanwhile, slice an andouille or another spicy cooked sausage into coins. Heat a fair amount of olive oil and brown the sausage; add a chopped onion, a chopped celery stalk, and a chopped green bell pepper and continue to cook until the vegetables begin to soften. Add some minced garlic, a tablespoon of chopped oregano (or a bit of dried), and enough flour to make a roux (add more oil if the mixture looks too dry). Turn the heat up so the roux browns quickly, but watch it like a hawk. As soon as it darkens and smells toasty add the pasta and enough of the pasta cooking water to keep everything moist. Toss well and garnish with chopped fresh parsley; break with tradition and serve with freshly grated Parmesan cheese if you like.

84.

Banderilla Pasta

This borrows the flavors of the original tapa to make a pasta sauce.

Boil salted water for pasta and cook it, reserving some of the cooking liquid. Meanwhile, chop a few crisp pickled peppers or pepperoncini, a handful of green olives, and a couple of good marinated artichoke hearts (optional). Using a fork, mash up a few anchovies (marinated in olive oil and packed in glass) and add them to the chopped vegetables. Toss the pasta with the vegetables and anchovies, adding a few tablespoons of the reserved liquid as needed to make a sauce; garnish with chopped olives or parsley.

85.

Pasta with Tomato Tapenade

You might crumble some fresh goat cheese over the top of this.

Boil salted water for pasta and cook it. Meanwhile, combine a half pound of pitted black olives in food processor with about a handful of drained capers, four or five anchovies, two cloves of garlic, freshly ground black pepper, and olive oil as needed to make a coarse paste. Put the tapenade in a large skillet over medium heat with several canned tomatoes, breaking them up as you cook, and stir until saucy, only a couple of minutes. Toss the pasta with just enough of the tapenade to gently coat the noodles. Serve with cheese if you like, passing any extra sauce at the table.

86.

Linguine with Butter, Parmesan, and Sage

The antecedent of "Alfredo" sauce, and much lighter (and I think better).

Boil salted water for pasta and cook it, leaving it just short of done and reserving some of the cooking liquid. Meanwhile, melt two tablespoons butter (or more) and add a couple handfuls of fresh sage leaves (about 30 leaves) to the pan; cook until the butter just browns and the leaves have shriveled. Add the pasta to the butter and sage, along with about three-quarters of a cup of the cooking liquid; cook until the pasta is done; it's OK if the mixture remains a little soupy. Stir in a couple of good handfuls of freshly grated Parmesan cheese and mix until it becomes creamy; season with lots of freshly ground black pepper and serve.

87.

Pasta with Chicken, Frisée, and Stilton

*Try playing with this combination of greens and cheese; use baby spinach
and feta or endive and goat cheese, for example.*

Boil salted water for pasta and cook it, reserving some of the cooking liquid. Meanwhile, cut a half pound or more of chicken cutlets into one-inch pieces. Chop an onion and cook it in some olive oil until it begins to soften, then add the chicken; sprinkle with salt and pepper and about a tablespoon of freshly chopped rosemary and cook for about four minutes. Separate a head of frisée. When the chicken is almost cooked through, add the frisée and cook until wilted, just a minute or so. Add the pasta to the chicken mixture, along with a handful of crumbled Stilton or another blue cheese. Add a couple tablespoons of the pasta water if needed to soften the cheese and moisten the sauce. Season with salt and pepper and garnish with toasted walnuts.

88.

Pasta with Walnut Pesto

Incredibly simple and incredibly rich.

Boil salted water for pasta and cook it, reserving some of the cooking liquid. Meanwhile, puree a cup of walnuts, some Parmesan cheese, a small handful of parsley, a few sage leaves, salt, pepper, and olive oil in a food processor; use just enough olive oil to get a nice, almost smooth consistency. Toss the pasta with the walnut sauce, using some of the reserved cooking water as needed to moisten it. Serve, topped with more freshly grated Parmesan cheese and some chopped parsley.

89.

Pasta with Garbanzo Beans, Sausage, and Arugula

One of my favorite "more sauce, less pasta" dishes.

Boil salted water for pasta and cook it, reserving some of the cooking liquid. Meanwhile, remove the casings from a couple of sweet Italian sausages and fry the meat, breaking it up into small pieces, until cooked through. Add a large can of drained, diced tomatoes, a can of drained chickpeas, a tablespoon of crushed fennel seeds, a good pinch of red chile flakes, salt, and pepper. Toss the pasta with a couple handfuls of arugula or another tender green (baby spinach, mizuna, and dandelion are all good) and let it wilt. Add the pasta to the sausage mixture, along with some pasta water if needed to moisten, and serve garnished with chopped parsley.

90.

Pasta with Bacon and Breadcrumbs

This relies on good breadcrumbs, which means homemade or panko.

Boil salted water for pasta and cook it, reserving some of the cooking liquid. Meanwhile, cut bacon into small pieces and fry it in a bit of olive oil until just crisping; remove from the pan and add two or three minced cloves of garlic to the pan; cook over fairly low heat, turning until just fragrant, a couple of minutes. Toss in a cup or so of breadcrumbs and a pinch of red chile flakes; cook, stirring, until the breadcrumbs turn golden (they go fast, so you'll want to watch them). Toss the pasta and the breadcrumb mixture along with the bacon and a little of the reserved liquid. Top with some more olive oil and a bit of chopped parsley or basil.

91.

Linguine with Pea Sauce and Prosciutto

Good when you're eager for a taste of spring. I don't bother to strain the sauce, but you can.

Boil salted water for pasta and cook it, reserving some of the cooking liquid. Meanwhile, cook a bag of frozen peas and a couple of chopped scallions in just enough salted, boiling water to cover everything; simmer until tender, just a couple of minutes. Puree most of the peas with as much cooking liquid as you need in a food processor or blender. Cut a few slices of prosciutto into matchsticks and cook for about two minutes or until coloring slightly; add the remaining whole peas to the prosciutto. Toss the pasta with the pea puree; mix in the prosciutto and whole peas. Season with lots of freshly ground pepper and salt to taste; serve with freshly grated Parmesan cheese.

92.

Warm Milk Toast

Day-old bread is ideal for this; it won't become soggy.

Warm two tablespoons of butter in a large pot; add a cup of milk, a quarter cup of raw cane sugar, and a quarter cup of raisins. Heat this mixture, stirring until the sugar melts, but don't bring it to a boil. Slice good-quality bread (brioche is nice) into two-inch cubes and put the bread in the pot; add as much bread as needed to soak up the milk without becoming soggy. Transfer everything to a bowl to serve; drizzle with a couple of tablespoons of dark rum or whiskey and sprinkle with cinnamon.

93.

Lemon Mascarpone Mousse

*Try substituting orange rind and juice for the lemon and add a touch
of Grand Marnier in place of the cream.*

Finely grate the rind of a lemon. Whisk together a cup of mascarpone, the lemon's juice
and grated rind, and about a quarter cup of sugar (or more to taste) until smooth. Add
a tablespoon or two of heavy cream to moisten if needed. If you have time, chill for a bit
before serving in pudding cups; top with a drizzle of honey and serve with ladyfingers.

94.

Candied Citrus Rinds

A combination of different citrus fruit makes for a gorgeous presentation.

Bring a small pot of water to a boil. Slice an orange, a grapefruit, or a lime into
quarters and remove the flesh from the peel. (Use it for whatever you like.) Slice
each quarter rind into quarter-inch-thick strips; boil for a minute, then remove from
the water with a slotted spoon. In a combination of one part sugar to one part water
boil the rinds a second time, for about five minutes. Drain, toss with a bit of sugar until
lightly coated, and set on a cookie sheet to dry. If you like, melt some dark chocolate
and dip the rinds halfway. Serve warm, alongside good butter cookies or shortbread.

95.

Grapefruit 'n' Cream Shake

*In spring and summer strawberries and tarragon are also a lovely combination,
though you may have to add a bit of water depending on how juicy your fruit is.*

In a blender, combine two cups of grapefruit juice, a half cup of cream, and a couple
tablespoons (or more) of sugar. Add a cup of ice and blend until it becomes a slushy
consistency. Serve immediately, garnished with a dusting of cayenne if you like.

96.

Whipped Grapefruit Cream with Chocolate Drizzle

The nuts (use whatever type you like) are optional, but they do add a nice crunch.

Melt four ounces of bittersweet chocolate. Whip two cups of heavy cream along with two tablespoons of fresh grapefruit juice and two tablespoons zest; continue whipping until stiff peaks form. Fold in a handful of chopped pistachios. Spoon the grapefruit cream into serving dishes, drizzle with the warm chocolate, and garnish with a sprig of mint.

97.

Orange Fool

You can let this chill and set, or serve immediately.

Combine one and one-half cups orange juice and two tablespoons orange zest in a medium saucepan; simmer gently over medium-low heat until reduced to half its original volume, about fifteen minutes. Meanwhile, whip one and one-half cups of heavy cream until soft peaks form, then add three tablespoons of powdered sugar and continue beating, forming stiff peaks. Cool the saucepan in an ice bath for a minute or two, then strain the orange reduction into the whipped cream. Add three-quarters cup unsweetened flaked coconut and fold gently to combine everything. Garnish with additional coconut.

98.

Almond Tart

Great for guests, as you can serve it hot or at room temperature.

Heat the broiler. In a medium bowl, mix together four eggs, one-third cup of sugar, one-half cup of ground almonds, three-quarters cup of half-and-half, and a half cup of blanched slivered almonds. Melt two tablespoons of butter and add the almond mixture to the pan; mix to evenly distribute the almonds and cover. Cook until the eggs are set; put the pan uncovered in the broiler for about two minutes or until just golden on top. Sprinkle with powdered sugar and additional almonds to serve.

99.

Aztec Hot Chocolate

Increase or decrease the amount of cayenne as you like.

Whip a half cup of heavy cream with a half teaspoon of cayenne pepper and one teaspoon of vanilla extract until soft peaks form; set aside. In a small pot, warm four cups of whole milk with a half cup of chopped semisweet chocolate, a bit more cayenne, and a half teaspoon of cinnamon. Warm the milk until it just begins to bubble (don't let it boil) and the chocolate is melted. Transfer the chocolate milk to mugs and top with the spicy whipped cream.

100.

Nutella Fondue

For fans of Nutella, this is heaven.

Warm a cup of Nutella with a cup of cream and mix to combine well. Cut your favorite bakery pound cake into cubes and slice a couple of not-too-ripe bananas. Use skewers to dip the pound cake and bananas into the fondue.

101.

Chocolate Chip Pancakes

Topped with rum-infused whipped cream, this breakfast favorite becomes a fabulous dessert.

In a bowl, mix together two cups of flour, two teaspoons baking powder, one-quarter teaspoon salt, one tablespoon sugar, two eggs, one and one-half cups milk, and two tablespoons oil or melted butter; some lumps can remain. Warm a large pan with a tablespoon or two of butter, ladle some batter into the pan, and sprinkle the batter with chocolate chips. When the pancake begins to bubble, flip and cook for another minute more or until golden brown.

Spring

We expect so much of spring,

and though it comes slowly, it brings lettuce and other greens, peas, asparagus, onions, rhubarb, strawberries, broccoli, turnips, beets, and more. After a long winter when almost every vegetable comes from the great Central Valley of California or even farther away, anything local is welcome.

We can do wonderful things with that produce as it becomes available. Everything mentioned above, along with spinach, escarole, endive, citrus, arugula, fennel, and more, makes its way into dishes that draw back the curtain of winter.

1.

Fried Eggs with Lemon and Chervil

Chervil, an herb that tastes like basil, can be hard to find, but tarragon and chives are fine substitutes.

Cook a little minced garlic in butter over medium heat until fragrant, then add a few tablespoons of lemon juice and cook a couple of minutes more. Gently add four eggs to the pan, cover, and cook until just set. Sprinkle with freshly chopped chervil and serve with crusty bread.

2.

Chilaquiles

To avoid frying fresh tortillas, use tortilla chips.

Cut corn tortillas (flour tortillas will do, but they're not as good) into strips. Fry in not too much oil—with a few chopped jalapeños, pickled or not, if you tend in that direction—until crisp, about three minutes, turning; drain on paper towels. Beat a few eggs with a bit of milk or cream and sprinkle with salt and pepper. Heat a tablespoon or so of the frying oil (save or discard the rest) and add the tortilla strips and eggs. Cook, stirring, until the eggs are done, two to four minutes. Garnish with salsa (or stir some salsa in there), chopped avocado, cheese, scallions, sour cream, or whatever else you like.

3.

Mixed Herb Omelet

A combo of thyme, basil, marjoram, and rosemary is also good.

Beat four eggs with two tablespoons of milk. Add a pinch of salt and pepper and a small handful of parsley and mint, along with smaller amounts of tarragon and thyme. Set a medium nonstick pan over medium-low heat and add butter to the pan, followed, a minute or two later, by the egg mixture. Cook, undisturbed, until the eggs are mostly set but still quite runny in the center. Fold the omelet in half, slide it from the pan, and serve topped with more chopped herbs.

4.

Hangtown Fry

Supposedly the breakfast of forty-niners (the gold miners, not the football team).

Cook about one-quarter pound of chopped bacon (slab is best) in a little olive oil over medium heat for a minute or two; add one-half cup mushrooms (shiitakes are good) if you like, and cook until brown, with salt and pepper. Add six or eight shucked oysters, cook for a half minute or so. Stir in four or five beaten eggs, with some parsley. Scramble soft and serve with toast.

5.

Eggs Bhona

Add as much or as little spice as you like to this Bangladeshi take on eggs dish.

Boil eight eggs for about six minutes; meanwhile, cook a chopped onion and a chopped green bell pepper in vegetable oil, just until soft. Add a crushed clove of garlic, one-quarter teaspoon each ground ginger and turmeric, a pinch each of red chile flakes and salt, a bay leaf, and a quarter cup of tomato paste and give a good stir. Then add a cup or so boiling water to make a sauce. Shell the eggs and add to the onion mixture. Cover and cook for five minutes.

6.

Lemongrass-and-Chicken Soup

You can add rice vermicelli or mung bean noodles to this if you like.

Heat chicken stock, about a cup-and-a-half per serving. Trim a stalk of lemongrass per serving; bruise the pieces with the back of a knife. Add the lemongrass and a few slices of ginger to the stock, along with two or three minced hot chiles, or to taste. After a few minutes, remove the lemongrass and ginger and add fish or soy sauce and chopped oyster mushrooms or any other mushrooms and some chunks of cooked chicken (or pork, beef, or cubed tofu). Season with lime juice (lots) and salt, and garnish with cilantro leaves.

7.

Udon Noodles with Green Tea Broth

You can embellish this with bonito flakes,
cucumber or avocado slices, chopped scallions, sesame seeds,
or shredded cooked beef or chicken.

Bring about two quarts of water to a boil in a large pot. Tie three tablespoons of green tea leaves in a piece of cheesecloth or put in a tea ball. Remove the pot from the heat and steep the tea for about five minutes or to desired strength. Discard the tea and return to a boil, adding a pinch of salt. Add eight ounces of udon noodles. Cook, stirring once or twice, until noodles are tender. Taste and add some more salt, pepper, and mirin or sugar if desired.

8.

Miso Soup with Tofu

For more substance, add a few chopped cooked shrimp or some shredded chicken.

Bring four or five cups of water to a boil. Whisk a cup of the water with a quarter cup of miso (more if you like) in a bowl until smooth. Pour the miso mix into the water and add cubed tofu, minced carrots, and minced scallions to serve with soy sauce on the side.

9.

Lime and Chicken Soup

Pretty much a perfect combination of flavors, as long as you're generous with both lime juice and cilantro.

Cut a couple boneless, skinless chicken breasts or thighs into one-half-inch chunks; brown in olive oil; then add a chopped onion, a smashed garlic clove, a pinch of cinnamon, and the zest of a lime; cook a minute or so. Add six cups chicken broth and bring to a boil. Stir in a chopped avocado and the juice from the lime. Serve, sprinkled with lots of cilantro, with tortilla chips on the side.

10.

Spinach and White Bean Soup

Any tender green is fine here; arugula, watercress, or dandelion adds a nice peppery flavor.

Cook half a chopped onion with a smashed clove of garlic in some olive oil for about three minutes. Add precooked or canned white beans (with their liquid) and about five cups of chicken or vegetable broth; bring to a boil. Reduce to a simmer and cook for about five minutes, mashing some of the beans a bit if you like. Add two or three cups of chopped spinach and one-quarter cup chopped parsley. Stir to wilt the greens and serve with a hunk of crusty bread and grated Parmesan.

11.

Asparagus Leek Soup

A nice combination of early spring ingredients.

Slice the white part of a leek and cook it for three to five minutes in a couple of tablespoons of butter or oil along with a smashed clove of garlic, a chopped carrot, and a bunch of chopped fresh asparagus. Add about six cups of chicken or vegetable stock and bring to a boil. Reduce to a simmer and cook until the vegetables are tender, five minutes or so. Puree the ingredients until smooth. You can add a few tablespoons of cream if you want a richer finish.

12.

Soup with Poached Eggs and Greens

It doesn't get much faster or better than this.

Bring six cups of vegetable or chicken stock to a slow bubble. Add two cups of any chopped tender greens (spinach, arugula, and mizuna all work well), then four shelled eggs, along with a couple of smashed cloves of garlic, some freshly grated Parmesan, and red chile flakes to taste. Cook until the whites of the eggs are set but the yolks still soft, about three minutes. Scoop out the garlic cloves if you care, and serve immediately.

13.

Chilled Cucumber and Dill Soup

The fresh dill is what makes this fabulous.

Peel and seed three cucumbers. Chop them up and put in a blender with two cups of buttermilk, a half cup of sour cream, a tablespoon of olive oil, a couple of tablespoons of freshly chopped dill, a pinch of sugar, salt, and a splash of white wine vinegar. Puree and garnish with fresh dill. Serve with crusty bread.

14.

Vietnamese Noodle Soup with Beef

I poach an egg or two in this soup at the end,
but you can also just add a couple of hard-boiled eggs.

Soak rice vermicelli and a handful of snow peas, cut in pieces if you like, in boiling water for about 10 minutes. Drain the noodle–snow pea combination in a colander and rinse with cold water; divide evenly among four bowls. Quickly cook a few slices of fresh ginger and a chopped chile, then add a quart of beef broth along with two cups of water and bring to a simmer. Divide one-half pound of thinly sliced rare roast beef among the four bowls (roast beef from a deli is fine, though leftovers are preferable), along with a few torn basil, cilantro, and mint leaves. Stir a tablespoon or so of Asian fish sauce and fresh lime juice into the simmering broth and ladle into bowls. Serve immediately.

15.

Fast Fish Soup

Not a true bouillabaisse, but a good and very fast knockoff.

In a couple tablespoons of olive oil, soften a chopped onion, a smashed clove of garlic, and half teaspoon paprika for about two minutes. Add four cups of stock (fish, vegetable, or chicken), a can of chopped-up tomatoes with their juice, a pinch of saffron, salt, and pepper; bring to a boil. Reduce to a simmer and cook for five minutes. Add about a pound or a pound-and-a-half of white fish, cut into chunks, to the stock; or a mix of scallops, shrimp, and well-washed clams, with some fish if you like. Simmer until the fish is cooked through, about five minutes more. Serve garnished with chopped parsley and slices of toasted baguette.

16.

Classic Caesar Salad

The quality of your anchovies will make a difference; use those marinated in olive oil and packed in glass.

Rub the inside of a large salad bowl (wooden, preferably) with a clove of garlic. Cook two eggs in gently boiling water for about a minute to a minute and a half (you want them barely coddled). Crack the eggs into the bowl and beat them as you add freshly squeezed lemon juice and a few tablespoons of olive oil. Stir in two or more anchovies (you can chop these first if you like), a dash or two of Worcestershire sauce, salt, and plenty of pepper. Toss with a chopped head of romaine, garnish with lots of freshly grated Parmesan, and serve with Italian bread or croutons.

17.

Salad Niçoise

The classic composed French salad made simple.

Boil and salt a pot of water. Chop a couple of potatoes (peeled or not) into half-inch dice and boil until a knife can be easily inserted, about eight minutes. When the potatoes are nearly done, add a handful of trimmed green beans or haricots verts and cook until crisp-tender, just a minute or two. Drain the vegetables and plunge them into ice water to stop the cooking process. Put a bunch of mixed baby greens in a bowl with the beans, the potatoes, a handful of good-quality black olives, a few chopped anchovies, a diced tomato, and half a sliced red onion. Combine one-quarter cup of olive oil, a few tablespoons of sherry vinegar, a teaspoon or so of Dijon mustard, salt, and pepper and dress the salad. Top the salad with a drained can of tuna packed in olive oil.

18.

Spinach Salad
with Smoked Trout and Apples

You can use either tart or sweet apples; just make sure they're crisp.

Toast a handful or two of sliced almonds in a dry skillet until just fragrant. Core two apples and cut them into thin slices. In a large bowl, whisk together a quarter cup of olive oil, the juice of a lemon, and a tablespoon of Dijon mustard. Add the apples and toss to coat. Break a smoked trout into bite-size pieces and add it to the bowl along with a mound of fresh spinach, the toasted almonds, and a handful of currants or raisins. Season with salt and pepper.

19.

Poached Eggs and Truffled Arugula
Prosciutto Salad

Real truffles are best, of course, but occasionally truffle oil can be nice;
you can also use good-quality extra-virgin olive oil here.

Sear a few slices of prosciutto on high heat to crisp them, about two minutes, then set it aside to drain on a paper towel. Poach four eggs in boiling water for about three minutes. Remove the eggs with a slotted spoon, draining off all the excess water, and set them on a large bed of arugula. Top the eggs with the prosciutto, crumbling it between your fingers. Sprinkle the salad with a few dashes of truffle oil, along with salt and pepper to taste.

20.

Carrot and Couscous Salad

An incredibly easy salad with North African flavors.

Add couscous to a pot of boiling water, turn off the heat, cover, and let sit for 10 minutes. Shred four or five carrots and mix them with the juice of a lemon, a few tablespoons of fresh orange juice, about one-quarter cup of olive oil, a bit of cumin, and salt and pepper. When the couscous is done, drain it if necessary, fluff it gently with a fork, and add it to the carrots along with a handful of raisins. Toss well and serve.

21.

Chive Salad

Add cooked chicken, shrimp, or tofu to make this a meal.

In a large salad bowl, whisk together equal parts soy sauce, water, and rice wine vinegar. Add a few drops of sesame oil and a pinch of sugar. Roughly chop a couple of bunches of chives and add them to the bowl along with some chopped romaine or iceberg lettuce. Toss well and serve.

22.

Asparagus and Sesame Salad

Thinner asparagus works better here; but be careful not to overcook the spears.

Trim a bunch of asparagus, then cut the spears on the bias. Cook them quickly in a bit of vegetable oil for a minute or two, or until they turn bright green (you can also blanch them quickly in boiling water). Toss the cooked spears with a tablespoon or two of sesame oil, a splash of rice vinegar, a drizzle of soy sauce, and a sprinkle of sugar if you like; garnish with toasted sesame seeds and chopped scallions.

23.

Seared Scallops with Escarole, Fennel, and Orange Salad

You can mix this up a bit by using grapefruit, tangerines, blood oranges, or any combination of sweet citrus.

In a large salad bowl, mix together about one-quarter cup olive oil, a few splashes of white wine or sherry vinegar, some salt and pepper, and the zest of an orange. Now peel the orange, getting as much pith off as you can, and divide the fruit into sections. Core and thinly slice a head of fennel and toss this into the bowl with a couple of cups of chopped escarole and the orange sections. Sear eight to 12 scallops in olive oil until nicely browned on both sides, sprinkling them with salt and pepper. Give the salad another good toss and serve the scallops on top.

24.

BLT Salad

The avocado dressing really sets this apart.

Fry a few small cubes of slab bacon for about five minutes or until crisp. Puree an avocado, a handful of basil leaves, a clove of garlic, juice from one—or more—limes, about one-quarter cup of olive oil, salt, and pepper together in a food processor or blender; if you like a thinner dressing, add a few drops of water. Mix a head of Bibb or romaine lettuce with sliced tomatoes and chopped red onions. Add the bacon to the vegetables and dress with the pureed mixture. Serve with warm, crusty bread.

25.

Spicy Pork Salad

For an even spicier version,
add a pinch or two of cayenne or red chile flakes to the rub.

Coat thin, boneless pork chops with a mixture of sugar, cumin, chili powder, and salt and set aside to marinate. Combine a few handfuls of baby spinach leaves with half a thinly sliced red pepper, sections of a navel orange, a sliced avocado, and a small handful of toasted pine nuts. Mix together some olive oil, a good squeeze of fresh lime and orange juices, a teaspoon of Dijon mustard, salt, and pepper to dress the salad. Grill, broil, or pan-cook the pork until it's just done; cut into strips; and serve on top of the vegetables with the dressing drizzled over all.

26.

Lebanese Potato Salad

Frozen favas are a lovely addition to the pot; allow a minute or two more cooking time.

Peel and chop four or five large Yukon Gold potatoes; put them in a pot, cover with salted water, bring to a boil, and cook until tender, adding about a cup of frozen peas during the last couple of minutes of cooking. Drain and run under cold water to stop the cooking. Transfer to a large bowl; dress with olive oil, freshly squeezed lemon juice, minced garlic, chopped parsley and scallions, salt, pepper, and coriander seeds if you like and toss to mix well. Serve warm, cold, or in between.

27.

Greek Stuffed Pita Bread

For a salad skip the pita and toss everything with lots of romaine.

Mix together about a cup of plain yogurt, some chopped fresh mint, lemon juice, salt, and pepper. Slice the pitas in half crosswise to create pockets. Stuff the pockets with chopped tomatoes, feta cheese, cucumbers, oil-cured black olives, and roasted red peppers (the ones from a jar are fine; drain them first). Top with a dollop or two of the yogurt mixture and serve.

28.

Green Papaya Salad, with Shrimp

Green papaya is just unripe papaya, easy enough to find.

Cook a dozen or more medium shrimp in a little vegetable oil. Meanwhile, combine a tablespoon of brown sugar, juice of a lime, a garlic clove, a tablespoon fish or soy sauce, one-half teaspoon chile flakes (more or less), and some peeled ginger in a blender or food processor and puree. Grate (the food processor is good for this) a peeled and seeded green papaya (not one the size of a football) and two carrots. Toss with shrimp, sliced fresh tomatoes, and dressing; season to taste; and top with chopped peanuts.

29.

Tuna and Bean Salad

Tuna packed in olive oil, from Europe, is the key here, as is good olive oil.

Mix a cup or so of precooked or canned cannellini beans (drained) with a can of good tuna, a handful of chopped parsley, salt, pepper, a teeny bit of garlic (optional) or shallot (or red onion, or scallion, or whatever), and, if you have it, a sprig of rosemary. Drizzle with olive oil, toss, adjust seasoning, and serve with good bread or alongside cold cooked asparagus.

30.

Curried Chicken Salad Sandwich

*Almost any fairly neutral-flavored cooked chicken is fine here,
or use store-bought rotisserie chicken.*

Combine a spoonful or two of plain yogurt and half a fresh chopped mango (it doesn't have to be too ripe) in a large bowl. Add a few squeezes of fresh lime juice and curry powder to taste. Season with salt and pepper. Add shredded chicken, along with fresh chopped scallions and cilantro. Taste and adjust the seasoning; if the mixture is too moist, add more chicken or vegetables; if it's too dry, add more yogurt. Spread the salad on rolls, add arugula or lettuce, and serve.

31.

"Potpie" Chicken Salad Sandwich

Shuck a half cup of fresh peas, or run frozen peas under warm water and drain. Whisk together one-quarter cup chopped parsley, one-quarter cup cream, one-quarter cup mayonnaise, two tablespoons cider vinegar, and some salt and pepper. Chop a stalk of celery, a couple of scallions, and a carrot; add them to the bowl along with two cups chopped cooked chicken and the peas. Stir to combine, moistening with more cream if needed. Serve on bread, rolls, or croissants.

32.

Minted Pea and Prosciutto Sandwich

An unbeatable combination.

Blanch half of a bag of frozen peas in salted, boiling water. Put the peas in a food processor or blender with a couple of tablespoons of olive oil, a handful each of grated Parmesan and chopped mint, salt, and pepper; puree until smooth. Spread the pea mixture onto toasted sourdough bread and layer with slices of prosciutto.

33.

Cheese "Burger"

*I'm not saying you'll never go back to meat, but these are intense. Keep 'em small,
and garnish freely; even traditional burger garnishes are fine.*

Combine two cups grated Parmesan cheese with a handful of chopped parsley and
about a cup good breadcrumbs (all of this can be done together in a food processor).
Add two beaten eggs and gently mold into thin patties. Heat olive oil and cook patties
until brown around the edges, about five minutes. Flip and cook the other side for
another three minutes. Serve with tomato sauce or on a bun with garnishes.

34.

Seared Chicken Arugula Rollups

If you feel inspired, include a slice of prosciutto in each roll.

Flatten some chicken tenders with your hand or the bottom of a pot, brush both
sides with olive oil, and sprinkle with salt and pepper. Crumble some Gorgonzola on
each and top with a couple of arugula leaves. Roll the chicken up tightly lengthwise
and secure with a toothpick. Warm some butter over medium-high heat and sear
rollups until browned on all sides, about six minutes. Serve with toasted baguette
slices rubbed with fresh garlic.

35.

Anchovy Egg Sandwich

Served open-face, this is pretty close to perfect.

Hard-boil four eggs. While they're cooking, smear a slice of rye toast with sour cream
or plain yogurt; top with sliced tomatoes and good-quality anchovies. When the eggs
are done, peel them and slice them onto the sandwich. Drizzle with olive oil and
garnish with fresh dill (a sprinkling of dried dill will work too).

36.

Middle Eastern Pizza

Also known as lahmacun.

Mix together about a half pound of ground lamb, a chopped onion, a chopped tomato (canned is fine), some minced garlic, a couple of tablespoons tomato paste, some chopped fresh mint, salt, and pepper. Spread a thin layer on pocketless pita or lavash bread; bake at 450°F for eight minutes, or until the lamb is fully cooked. Sprinkle with lemon juice and serve.

37.

Italian Tostada

OK, it's not traditional, but it's pretty good, like an extremely thin-crust pizza.

Heat the oven to 400°F. Brush flour tortillas with olive oil and bake until firmed up a bit. Evenly spread thinly sliced mozzarella cheese (preferably fresh), some chopped tomato, and slices of prosciutto on top. Bake again until the cheese melts. Drizzle a bunch of arugula with olive oil and lemon juice. Add the greens to the top of the tostadas and put them back in the oven for about a minute to gently wilt. Serve whole or sliced like a pizza.

38.

Chickpea Burgers

If you like hummus, this is your kind of burger.

Drain a can of chickpeas and put them in a food processor with a chopped shallot or some onion, a bit of oregano, paprika, salt, and an egg. Pulse the mixture until it's slightly grainy but even in consistency. Add enough flour—about a quarter cup—so you can form the mixture into flat burger patties. Sear them in olive oil until golden, about four minutes per side. Serve on good whole grain bread or a bun with tahini (optional), greens, and a squeeze of lemon juice.

39.

Saag Paneer

If you can't find paneer (an Indian cheese), use feta or tofu, which both work wonderfully.

Cut about a cup-and-a-half of paneer, feta, or firm tofu into half-inch cubes and chop a pound of spinach. Cook some minced garlic and ginger in peanut oil or another oil, along with a pinch or two of red chile flakes until soft, about two minutes. Stir in curry powder to taste (at least a tablespoon), along with some salt and pepper; add the spinach and cook until it wilts. Stir in a dusting of flour (use chickpea flour if you have it) and cook until just turning golden. Add a couple of spoonfuls of plain yogurt and a cup of half-and-half or cream; cook gently until the mixture begins to dry out. Add the paneer, feta, or tofu, and continue cooking until warmed through; add more half-and-half or cream if necessary, adjust the seasonings, and serve.

40.

Ketchup-Braised Tofu with Veggies

You can use sugar snap peas or asparagus tips instead of green beans.

Press extra-firm tofu between layers of paper towels for a few minutes, or longer if you have time; cut into one-inch squares. Heat a few tablespoons of vegetable oil in a skillet and sear the tofu until golden and crisp, turning once or twice. Add about one-quarter cup of ketchup, a dash of rice vinegar, a few drops of sesame oil, and enough water to make a little sauce. Stir in a thinly sliced carrot, a couple of handfuls of green beans, and a pinch of red chile flakes. Cover the skillet and reduce the heat; braise for about four minutes or until the vegetables are just tender. At the last minute, toss in a handful of bean sprouts or shredded cabbage, give a good stir, and serve, with soy sauce on the side.

41.

Snap Peas with Walnuts and Roquefort

You can also use slender haricots verts here if you can find them.

Cook about a pound of snap peas in salted, boiling water until crisp-tender, about a minute. Drain and shock in ice water to stop the cooking. Soften a minced shallot in olive oil until it's translucent, for another minute or so. Add a handful of chopped walnuts and cook until fragrant, about another minute. Add the peas, salt, and pepper and warm through. Serve with Roquefort cheese crumbled on top.

42.

Spicy Stir-fried Bean Sprouts

Try starting this dish with ground pork, chicken, minced shrimp or tempeh,
or crumbled tofu.

Heat a film of peanut or vegetable oil in a deep skillet and add a mound of bean sprouts with minced fresh ginger and a bit of minced chile if you like; toss to coat with oil. Cook, stirring, for about three minutes, then add a couple of tablespoons of any spice blend (Chinese five-spice, curry powder, etc.) and some salt and pepper. Add a few drops of water if the sprouts begin to stick. Cook another minute. Serve with leaves of romaine or Boston lettuce and make little bundles of the sprouts.

43.

Crisp Fennel Gratin

Heat the broiler and bring a pot of water to a boil. Cut a couple of fennel bulbs into quarter-inch-thick slices and boil for about three minutes or until just tender. Drain and put in a shallow broiler-safe dish; top with a layer of breadcrumbs (homemade are better) and freshly grated Parmesan cheese. Put the dish under the broiler for about three minutes or until the cheese melts and the breadcrumbs are golden. Garnish with some of the chopped fennel fronds if you like.

44.

Broccoli Rabe and Couscous

To add a bit of heft, crumble some cooked Italian sausage (sweet, hot, or a combination) in with the broccoli rabe.

Boil two pots of water. When the first is ready, add the couscous, turn off the heat, cover, and let it sit for 10 minutes. Salt the second pot of water and blanch a bunch of broccoli rabe for about two minutes, until crisp-tender; drain well and chop. When the couscous is done, drain if necessary and fluff it with a fork. Add the rabe along with a few tablespoons of olive oil, some freshly squeezed lemon juice, salt, and pepper. Mix to combine; top with freshly grated Parmesan and serve.

45.

Seared Fish with Lettuce Leaves

Use anything sustainable, good, fresh, and firm.

Warm a couple of tablespoons of sesame oil (or use olive or peanut oil; something with flavor, in any case) in a skillet over medium-high heat. Sprinkle fish chunks with salt and pepper and sear until just done. Wrap at the table in leaves of Boston or other tender lettuce, or grape leaves from a jar, garnished with lemon juice and fresh mint or lime juice and basil, mint, and/or cilantro.

46.

Fish in Spicy Soy Sauce

This easy, useful sauce can work with virtually any fish.

Combine one-quarter cup of soy sauce, one-quarter cup of water, a large pinch of sugar, a couple of chopped scallions, and a diced chile in a deep skillet; bring to a boil. Add the fish and adjust the heat so that the mixture bubbles gently. Cook for about eight minutes, depending on the thickness of the fish, turning it once or twice gently until it's coated with the sauce. Spoon on the sauce, garnish with chopped scallions, and serve.

47.

Fish Braised in Lemon
with Tomatoes and Red Peppers

Try sprinkling a few capers on top of the fish just before serving.

Thinly slice a medium onion and a red pepper, then cook them in olive oil; once they soften, add a handful of cherry tomatoes or grape tomatoes, cut in half. Season any white-fleshed fish with salt and pepper; move the vegetables to the side of the pan and sear the fish for about two minutes. Turn, add freshly squeezed lemon juice, then cover and simmer for another three minutes, or until the fish is cooked through (this may take longer, depending on the thickness of the fish). Adjust the seasonings and serve the fish topped with the vegetables and freshly chopped parsley.

48.

Prosciutto-Wrapped Fish
with Wilted Greens

The prosciutto provides a wonderfully crisp crust to the tender fish,
which can be any white-flesh fish.

Heat the oven to 400°F. Season fish fillets with salt and pepper and wrap them in thin slices of prosciutto (it'll stick to itself, but no problem). In a tablespoon each of butter and olive oil, cook the fish for about two minutes on each side or until the prosciutto begins to color and crisp up; put the fish in the oven and continue cooking until done, another five minutes or so. Cook some minced garlic in olive oil and add a bunch of spinach or other tender greens until just wilted; season with salt and pepper. Serve the fish on top of the greens.

49.

Fish with Edamame Pesto

Blanch a bag's worth of edamame for three to five minutes. Put the beans in a blender with a few tablespoons of olive oil or more, as needed to get a nice puree; a handful of grated Parmesan cheese; and a clove or two of garlic. Blend until smooth and season with salt and pepper. Season any fish fillets or steaks with salt and pepper and cook them in a couple of tablespoons of butter or olive oil for about four minutes on each side or until golden and cooked through. Serve the fish with a spoonful of the pesto and garnished with roughly chopped walnuts.

50.

Seared Fish with Fennel and Orange

More delicate fish are best in this recipe.

Slice a bulb of fennel very thinly (a mandoline works best). Peel two large oranges and segment them. Sprinkle four fish fillets with salt and pepper; dredge in flour, a beaten egg, and then panko. Sear in a mixture of olive oil and butter, turning once until both sides are golden and the fish is cooked through. Mix together a few tablespoons of olive oil, some freshly squeezed lemon juice, salt, and pepper. Drizzle the dressing on the fennel and orange slices and serve alongside the fish.

51.

Cajun-Style Salmon

A flexible rub that will boost the flavor of almost any grilled fish.

Mix together one teaspoon each paprika, coriander, cumin, and dried oregano; one-quarter teaspoon each cayenne and cinnamon; and some salt and pepper. Rub the mixture on salmon fillets and grill or broil on each side for four minutes, or to the desired doneness. Serve the salmon over a bed of mixed greens and garnish with lemon wedges.

52.

Fish with Thai "Pesto"

Use this herb paste on almost any seafood, chicken, or meat; it also works beautifully tossed with noodles.

In a food processor or blender, combine a few good handfuls of Thai basil, some cilantro, a few tablespoons of olive or vegetable oil, a fresh Thai chile, a clove of garlic, and a sprinkle of salt and pepper. Puree until nearly smooth, adding a bit more oil if needed. Season the fish with salt, pepper, and a pinch of cayenne. Heat a couple of tablespoons of butter or oil and cook the fish, turning once, until both sides are golden and the fish is cooked through. Top the fish generously with the pesto and serve.

53.

Crisp Fish with Citrus-Soy Glaze and Wilted Cress

Use any tender green you like here—arugula, mizuna, watercress, and dandelion all add a nice spice.

Stir together two teaspoons sugar, a teaspoon of water, and a couple of tablespoons each of grapefruit juice, lime juice, and soy sauce. Heat a couple of tablespoons of extra-virgin olive oil in a pan and cook any sturdy fish fillets (skin side down, if they have skin) for about two minutes, until crispy. Flip fillets and cook them for another minute; add the citrus-soy mixture and swirl gently until it's reduced to a glaze and the fish is cooked through. In another pan heat a tablespoon or so of olive oil; add a bunch of watercress, sprinkle with salt, and toss until just wilted. Serve the glazed fish over a bed of the wilted cress.

54·
Garlic-Ginger Shrimp

*Fast and fragrant; you can save time by using the tip of a teaspoon
to peel the ginger and a microplane to grate it.*

Cook some grated or minced ginger and garlic in a couple of tablespoons of vegetable oil. Add a pound of shrimp to the pan, along with one-quarter cup of rice or dry white wine; cook until the shrimp turn pink on both sides and are no longer translucent, about three minutes. Add chopped scallions, toss, and serve over noodles.

55·
Mark's Famous Spicy Shrimp

*The best "bring-to-the-grill-party" dish ever,
in my humble opinion; I've been doing it for 25 years.*

Use the side of a knife, a small food processor, or a mortar and pestle to make a paste from a couple of minced garlic cloves, salt, a pinch or two of cayenne, and about a tablespoon each of good paprika or pimentón, olive oil, and lemon juice. Smear the paste all over a pound or so of shrimp. Grill or broil the shrimp for about two minutes on each side and serve with lemon wedges.

56.
Shrimp with Asparagus, Dill, and Spice

Dried dill works just fine here.

Melt a few tablespoons of butter in a skillet; when it's hot, add about a pound of sliced asparagus; stir and cook until crisp-tender, about five minutes, then remove. Add some more butter to the pan and repeat with about a pound of shrimp, cooking until it turns pink, about four minutes. Return the asparagus to the pan and sprinkle with a few drops of Tabasco sauce, Worcestershire sauce, dill, and lemon juice. Serve over a bed of jasmine rice.

57.

Seared Scallops with White Wine and Chile

A handful of toasted breadcrumbs or slivered blanched almonds makes a nice garnish.

Slice scallops in half along their flat side. Soften some minced garlic and a chopped seeded chile in olive oil for about two minutes and remove. Sear the scallops, turning once. Remove the scallops from the pan and add about a half cup of white wine to the pan along with the garlic and chile mixture, and reduce quickly over high heat. Serve the scallops over pasta, rice, or toasted bread drizzled with the wine reduction (and a bit of good-quality olive oil if needed). Garnish with chopped parsley.

58.

Scallops with Sesame Seeds and Scallions

Toast sesame seeds in a dry skillet for just a minute or two: they're done when fragrant and golden. Remove. Then heat a couple of tablespoons of olive oil in the skillet and add the scallops, sprinkle with salt and pepper, and cook for two minutes or until lightly browned and opaque inside; set aside. Turn the heat up and add one-half stick of butter and one-half cup of dry white wine; continue stirring, scraping up the brown bits from the bottom of the pan and reducing until the sauce is thickened a bit. Add some chopped scallions and a splash of soy sauce and cook for another 30 seconds. Serve the scallops drizzled with the sauce and garnished with the toasted sesame seeds.

59.

Mussels with Green Curry and Cellophane Noodles

*Canned coconut milk is a wonderful thing, and the light versions,
which are lower in fat, do just fine here.*

Cover the noodles with boiling water and set aside. In a large pot, combine one-quarter cup water, the rind and juice of a lime, a teaspoon or so of sugar, a couple of tablespoons of green curry paste (or to taste), a splash of fish sauce, a can of coconut milk, and two to four pounds of mussels; bring to a boil. Cover and cook for about five minutes or until all the shells are open; discard any that don't open. Stir in a handful of chopped cilantro. Drain the noodles and serve the mussels and sauce on top.

60.

Chicken with Chilaquiles and Green Salsa

Store-bought green salsa is OK, but homemade takes just a couple of minutes.

Puree about a dozen tomatillos (canned are fine) with a large clove of garlic, a handful of fresh cilantro, lime juice, salt, and fresh chile to taste. Stir together a cup of sour cream with just enough milk so it can be poured. Bring a cup or so of the salsa to a boil over medium heat. Add a few handfuls of shredded chicken (leftover or from a store-bought rotisserie chicken), season with salt and pepper, and cook until the chicken is warmed through. Add a few handfuls of tortilla chips and let them soften for about a minute. Serve in bowls garnished with cilantro and more tortilla chips, and drizzled with the sour cream mixture. Pass any leftover salsa around the table.

61.

Chicken Tandoori

Perfect for skewers.

Heat the grill or broiler. In a bowl or dish large enough to hold the chicken, combine a cup of plain yogurt, a teaspoon each minced ginger and garlic, a teaspoon of paprika, a teaspoon cumin, a half teaspoon turmeric, the juice of a lime, and some salt and pepper. Marinate a pound of boneless, skinless chicken in this mixture for about five minutes. Grill or broil the chicken for about three minutes per side or until lightly browned and cooked through. Garnish with fresh cilantro and serve with basmati rice.

62.

Mediterranean Chicken

If you can find preserved lemons, a staple in Moroccan cooking, add some with the parsley.

Pound chicken breasts to one-quarter-inch thickness; sprinkle with salt and pepper and dredge in flour. Heat a few tablespoons of olive oil over medium-high heat and brown the chicken on both sides, about a minute per side, then remove. Stir a small handful of brine-cured green olives into the pan, along with a tablespoon of capers. Add a cup of chicken stock or white wine and bring to a boil; continue cooking over high heat until the liquid is reduced and syrupy, about four minutes. Finish with a couple of tablespoons of butter and chopped parsley and sprinkle with salt and pepper. Return the chicken to the sauce to heat through, then serve sprinkled with more chopped parsley.

63.

Spicy Chicken with Lemongrass and Lime

If you can find galangal (not always easy), it's a fun change from the ginger.

In a food processor, puree half an onion, a clove of garlic, a chunk of peeled ginger, the tender core from a stalk of lemongrass, a pinch of red chile flakes (or more if you like), and a teaspoon each of turmeric, sugar, and ground coriander, until a thick paste forms. Heat a couple of tablespoons of vegetable oil in a skillet; sear pounded chicken cutlets or tenders on both sides until brown. Remove the chicken from the pan and set aside; add the paste to the pan and cook for about two minutes. Return the chicken tenders to the pan and add half a cup of water or chicken stock; cover and simmer about four minutes. Serve the chicken with the sauce.

64.

Panko Chicken with Grapefruit-Honey Sauce

The sweetness of the honey, acidity of the grapefruit, and crunch of the panko really make this special.

Pound chicken breasts to one-quarter-inch thickness; dredge them first in a beaten egg and then in panko breadcrumbs seasoned with salt and pepper. Heat a few tablespoons of olive oil; cook the chicken on both sides until golden and just done, about four minutes total. Wipe the pan clean and soften some minced garlic for a minute in some more oil or butter; add half a cup of grapefruit juice and a tablespoon or so of honey. Season with salt and pepper and reduce until syrupy. Serve the chicken generously drizzled with the sauce and garnished with fresh grapefruit slices.

65.

Pan-Fried Herbed Chicken

Fresh herbs are the key here.

In a food processor, combine a small onion, two cloves of garlic, a tablespoon each of tarragon and sage, the juice of a lemon, a tablespoon of tahini or peanut butter, and a quarter cup of olive oil; puree until smooth. Rub the pureed mixture over boneless, skinless chicken pounded to half-inch thickness; dredge in flour. Fry the chicken in hot olive oil for about four minutes on each side, until well browned and cooked through. Serve over a mixed green salad with fresh lemon wedges on the side.

66.

Chicken with Green Olives

Good-quality European olives (think Greek or Spanish) are what you want here.

Pound chicken breasts to one-quarter-inch thickness. Heat a couple of tablespoons of butter or olive oil in a skillet and sear the chicken on both sides, about a minute per side; remove and set aside. Add to the pan half a diced onion, a teaspoon of minced or grated ginger, some minced garlic, and a half teaspoon each of ground cinnamon, cumin, and paprika. Cook until the onion softens, about three minutes. Add a half cup of chicken stock to the pan and bring to a boil; reduce to a simmer and return the chicken to the pan along with a handful of green olives, pitted and chopped. Continue cooking until the chicken is done, about two more minutes. Serve the chicken topped with the olives and drizzled with the sauce.

67.

Chicken with Almonds and Spinach

*A microwave comes in handy here to steam the spinach
and save dirtying an extra pan.*

Wash and chop a bunch of spinach and steam it; set aside. Pound chicken cutlets to about one-quarter-inch thickness; sprinkle with salt and pepper. Melt a couple of tablespoons of butter over medium-high heat and sear the chicken on each side until golden brown, about a minute per side. Add a couple of large minced cloves of garlic and arrange the steamed spinach and a handful of chopped almonds around the chicken, drizzling with more olive oil if you like; cover and cook for another minute or so until the chicken is done and everything is warmed through.

68.

Lemon Parmesan Chicken

Utterly simple yet sublime.

In a bowl, combine the grated rind from a large lemon, a cup of breadcrumbs (homemade are ideal), about a quarter cup of freshly grated Parmesan cheese, chopped fresh parsley, and some salt and pepper. Pound chicken cutlets to about a quarter-inch thickness; dredge in a beaten egg and the breadcrumb mixture. Cook the crusted cutlets in a couple of tablespoons of butter or olive oil over medium-high heat until golden on both sides and cooked through. Serve with lemon slices.

69.

Chicken Satay with Peanut Sauce

Homemade peanut sauce takes less than five minutes to make.

Pound chicken breasts to half-inch thickness and slice them into four-inch pieces. In a bowl, combine the juice from one lime with a smashed clove of garlic; add the chicken and let it marinate for five minutes. Meanwhile, whisk together a half cup of peanut butter, a couple of tablespoons of freshly squeezed lime juice, a splash of soy sauce, a pinch or two of red chile flakes, a teaspoon of brown sugar, and enough chicken broth or water to make a smooth sauce; adjust the seasoning. Set aside most of the sauce for dipping and smear the rest on the chicken pieces with a little salt and pepper, thread onto skewers, and grill for two minutes on each side or until cooked through. Serve with the reserved peanut sauce and lime wedges.

70.

Chicken with Coconut and Lime

You might thread the chicken onto skewers, then serve the coconut-lime mixture as a dipping sauce.

Heat the broiler. Cut boneless, skinless chicken into four-inch pieces and toss with the juice of a lime. Heat a can of coconut milk along with a pinch of cayenne, the zest of two limes, and the juice of the other lime. Broil the chicken for about six minutes, turning once, until browned and cooked through. Add about a teaspoon of fish sauce to the coconut milk and season with salt and pepper. Serve the sauce over the chicken and top with chopped scallions and sprinkled with freshly chopped cilantro.

71.

Moroccan Spiced Chicken with Yogurt Sauce

A bed of couscous completes this Moroccan-inspired meal.

Heat the broiler or a grill pan. Rub thin chicken breasts with a mixture of ground cumin, coriander, cayenne, cinnamon, salt, and pepper. Cook the chicken until nicely browned and done, turning once, six to eight minutes total. Mix a cup or so of plain yogurt with a couple of tablespoons of freshly squeezed lemon juice, some chopped fresh mint, and salt to taste. Serve the spice-rubbed chicken with the yogurt sauce and top with more mint and a slice of lemon.

72.

Vietnamese Caramelized Grilled Pork

This caramel sauce does wonders for shrimp as well; just thread the shrimp on skewers, drizzle with the sauce, and grill.

Pound boneless pork chops to quarter-inch thickness and heat the grill or broiler. In a small, heavy saucepan, combine half a cup of sugar with two tablespoons of water and stir with some grated ginger to make a paste; cook, undisturbed, over medium heat until it turns golden. Add a couple of finely diced shallots, a tablespoon each fresh lime juice and fish sauce, and a pinch of salt (at this point the caramel will harden); continue to cook, stirring constantly, until the caramel dissolves and the shallots are soft, about two minutes. Put the pork on the grill and brush with sauce, turning frequently until the chops are just cooked through.

73.

Beef and Corn Tacos

Unless corn is already in season, this is a good time to go with frozen.

Cook a chopped onion and a diced jalapeño pepper for a couple of minutes, until the onion starts to soften. Add a teaspoon each of chili powder and cumin (or more to taste) and cook for another 30 seconds. Add a pound or so of ground beef to the pan, sprinkle with salt and pepper, and cook through, about four minutes. Meanwhile, chop a tomato and an avocado; grate a cup or so of Jack or cheddar cheese. Add a few handfuls of corn to the meat mixture and continue to cook. Warm corn or flour tortillas and serve by wrapping some of the beef-corn mixture and the other fresh ingredients in each tortilla. Garnish with fresh cilantro and sour cream.

74.

Broiled Steak
with Fennel and Shallots

Fennel fronds make a lovely garnish.

Heat the broiler. Trim and slice a fennel bulb into about six wedges (save the fronds for later) and a few shallots into halves or wedges; toss with olive oil, salt, and pepper. Put the vegetables on one side of a broiler-safe pan; sprinkle one or two three-quarter-inch-thick boneless rib eye steaks with salt and pepper and put them on the other side of the pan. Broil for six to eight minutes, turning the steaks and vegetables halfway through cooking. Serve the steaks topped with the vegetables.

75.

Carne Cruda

A rare treat (OK, pun intended).

Cut a pound of filet mignon into quarter-inch cubes and combine in a bowl with a handful each of arugula and parsley, about one-quarter cup of olive oil, and a few tablespoons of freshly squeezed lemon juice. Season with salt and pepper and more lemon juice if needed. Serve with crusty bread.

76.

Steak with Butter and Ginger

Use more ginger here if you like.

Sprinkle one or two three-quarter-inch-thick boneless rib eyes with salt and pepper and sear the steaks in a hot skillet for about two minutes on each side; set aside. Add a couple of tablespoons of butter to the pan to melt; add about a tablespoon of fresh minced or grated ginger, a splash of soy sauce, and a bit of water (to keep the soy from burning); cook for about 30 seconds. Return the steaks to the pan and cook for another few minutes on each side, until done the way you like. Spoon the ginger sauce over the meat, and garnish with fresh cilantro.

77.

Stuffed Burgers

Try this with some sautéed mushrooms on top.

Season a pound or so of ground beef with a good pinch of dill (a handful if it's fresh), salt, and pepper; form the meat into patties (two patties per burger, so make them on the thin side). Put a slice of tomato and some cheese (Gruyère, cheddar, blue, whatever) on one patty and then use a second patty to cover the stuffing—making a sandwich of the patties. Pinch the sides of the burgers together to seal them. Cook the burgers on a hot grill, on a grill pan, or under the broiler, turning them once, until done.

78.

Lamb Kibbe

*Pine nuts and breadcrumbs replace bulgur for a nice twist on this
Middle Eastern–style dish.*

In a food processor, blend a handful of toasted pine nuts, about a cup of breadcrumbs, a half teaspoon of allspice, a teaspoon of cumin, and half a diced onion until everything reaches an even, grainy consistency. Combine this mixture in a bowl with about a pound of ground lamb and a couple of tablespoons of olive oil; form into golf-ball-size balls and flatten a bit into patties. Fry each patty for about three minutes per side, or until crisp and cooked through. Serve with pita bread, shredded lettuce, plain yogurt, and a squeeze of fresh lemon juice.

79.

Lamb "Gyro"

Great using chicken, too.

Cut lamb (preferably shoulder; leg is OK) into two-inch chunks. In a large bowl, combine a teaspoon each dried thyme, and ground cumin and coriander; a tablespoon of minced garlic; and a pinch of red chile flakes. Add the lamb and toss to coat well. Sear the lamb pieces in olive oil until browned on all sides. In a separate pan, cook a sliced onion and a sliced red pepper in olive oil, until just soft. Serve the lamb with the onions and pepper in a pita (or wrapped in fresh lavash bread) with a dash of hot sauce, topped with plain yogurt.

80.

Spring Lamb

Israeli couscous takes longer to cook but makes a nice change if you have the time.

Heat the broiler. Puree together a handful each of fresh mint and basil, a clove of garlic, a teaspoon of cumin, a pinch of cinnamon, and a few tablespoons of olive oil to make a paste. Sprinkle salt and pepper on lamb steaks (from leg or shoulder), pound to half-inch thickness, and coat with the herb paste. Broil the steaks, turning once, until done, about eight minutes. In the meantime, mix a cup of plain yogurt with half a diced red onion and chopped cucumber. Serve the lamb over couscous; top with the yogurt mixture.

81.

Pan-Fried Veal Cutlets

Classic, and perfect served with greens cooked in lots of garlic.

Season veal cutlets with salt and pepper; dredge the cutlets in flour, beaten egg, and breadcrumbs. Heat a few tablespoons of olive oil in a large pan and fry the cutlets over high heat, turning once, until golden and cooked through, about three minutes. Serve with lemon wedges and chopped parsley.

82.

Orzo "Risotto" with Chives

Use this technique for any herb or vegetable.

Heat a mixture of butter and olive oil until foamy; stir in a handful or two of chopped chives and some salt and pepper and cook until the herbs are softened and fragrant. Now stir in a pound of orzo and keep cooking and stirring until it begins to get translucent. Stir in chicken stock (or water), a ladleful at a time, waiting for the pan to get almost dry before adding another. Repeat until the pasta is al dente and most of the liquid is absorbed, about eight minutes. Add butter, grated Parmesan cheese, and enough stock to reach the consistency you like. Serve, passing more cheese at the table.

83.

Pasta with Anchovies and Breadcrumbs

Fresh breadcrumbs (as usual) are superior to store-bought, with more flavor and better texture.

Boil and salt water for pasta, and cook it. Meanwhile, heat a couple of tablespoons of olive oil in a pan and lightly toast a cup or so of breadcrumbs until just golden; set aside. Heat a bit more oil and add a pinch of red chile flakes and a few drained, chopped anchovies (the kind marinated in oil and packed in glass) and cook for a minute or so, smashing up the anchovies with a fork as they cook. Drain the pasta, reserving some of the cooking water. Add the pasta to the anchovy mix and toss, adding pasta water as needed to moisten the mixture into a sauce. Add the toasted breadcrumbs and—optionally—freshly grated Parmesan.

84.

Pasta with Moroccan Tapenade

European tuna, packed in oil, is essential here.

Boil and salt water for pasta, and cook it. Meanwhile, in a food processor, combine a couple of handfuls of pitted green olives, a few tablespoons of capers, a drained can of tuna, a couple of cloves of garlic, a teaspoon cumin, freshly ground black pepper to taste, and olive oil as necessary to get a coarse paste. Put the tapenade in a bowl; drain the pasta, reserving some of the cooking water. Add the pasta to the tapenade, tossing to coat; add pasta water or olive oil as needed to make a sauce.

85.

Pasta Carbonara

Pancetta, guanciale, or bacon will do the trick equally well here.

Boil and salt water for pasta, and cook it. Meanwhile, cut about a quarter pound of pancetta into small pieces and fry in a bit of olive oil until golden. In a bowl large enough to hold the pasta, beat together three eggs, about a half cup of freshly grated Parmesan cheese, and the meat. Drain the pasta, reserving some of the cooking water. Toss the pasta quickly with the egg mixture to combine (the heat from the pasta will cook the eggs); add a few tablespoons of pasta water if needed to moisten. Season with salt and lots of freshly ground black pepper; garnish with chopped parsley and more Parmesan to taste.

86.

Pasta with Lemon Sauce

*You might toss in a few shrimp or scallops,
or add a couple handfuls of steamed asparagus tips or peas.*

Boil and salt water for pasta, and cook it. Meanwhile, in a large pan, combine a half stick of butter, a half cup of cream, and a quarter cup of freshly squeezed lemon juice. When the butter melts, remove the pan from the heat and set aside. Drain the pasta and add it to the reserved lemon sauce and toss. Add a few teaspoons of grated lemon zest and freshly grated Parmesan. Garnish with chopped parsley or chives and serve.

87.

Arugula and Prosciutto Pasta

*Other greens can also be used here as long as they're tender enough
to wilt quickly when mixed with the pasta.*

Boil and salt water for pasta, and cook it. Meanwhile, sear a few pieces of prosciutto, chopped, until crisp, about two minutes. In a large bowl, mix together about one-half cup crumbled goat cheese, two cups of chopped arugula, and a few tablespoons of olive oil. Drain the pasta, reserving some of the cooking water. Add the hot pasta to the bowl, wilting the arugula and coating the noodles with the cheese and oil; add pasta water as needed to moisten. Season with salt and pepper and crumble the prosciutto over the top of the pasta to serve.

88.

Rice Noodles with Cilantro Pesto

A little nod to fusion cuisine.

Soak rice vermicelli in boiling water to cover. In a food processor, puree two large handfuls of cilantro, the juice of a lime, a few tablespoons of olive oil, a slice of soft butter, salt, and pepper. Toast a handful of peanuts in a skillet lightly until fragrant and just golden. Drain the noodles and toss with the cilantro pesto; garnish with the toasted nuts.

89.

Shrimp Pad Thai

Use leftover chicken instead of shrimp
if you like; just toss it in with the noodles at the end.

Boil and salt water for pasta and cook a pound of wide rice noodles (they take only a couple of minutes); drain, rinse, and set aside in a bowl of cold water. Dice a couple of green onions and a clove of garlic. In a small bowl, combine a tablespoon of sugar, a few tablespoons of fish sauce, a pinch or two of red chile flakes, and a couple of tablespoons of sesame oil. In a tablespoon or two of vegetable oil, cook a handful of shrimp until just cooked; set aside. Add a bit more oil to the pan and scramble two eggs. Add the shrimp, drained noodles, garlic, onions, a handful of bean sprouts, and the sugar mixture to the pan and cook until warmed through. Sprinkle with chopped peanuts and serve.

90.

Udon Noodles with Seafood and Soy-Lemon Sauce

Udon and soba both work equally well here.

Cook the udon noodles; drain, saving some of the cooking water. Cook about a pound of peeled shrimp or firm white fish in a little sesame oil until just opaque. Stir in about one-quarter cup freshly squeezed lemon juice, a couple of tablespoons of soy sauce, a tablespoon grated ginger, and a minced garlic clove. Add the noodles and enough cooking liquid to make a sauce. Sprinkle the noodles with a pinch of red chile flakes and fresh cilantro.

91.

Cheesy Semolina with Asparagus

Like polenta, only faster.

Bring two cups salted water to a boil with one-half cup milk. Meanwhile, thinly slice a bunch of asparagus spears on the diagonal. When the water boils, whisk in one cup semolina and a pat of butter, cooking and stirring for three minutes; then add the asparagus and some grated Parmesan. Cover and set aside for a few minutes, until the vegetables are crisp-tender. Give a good stir and serve, garnished with more cheese, some chopped mint, and lots of freshly ground black pepper.

92.

Herbed Fresh Cheese Patties

Lovely over a bed of greens.

Dice half an onion and cook it in a tablespoon or so of olive oil until just soft. Using doubled cheesecloth, squeeze all the moisture out of two cups of ricotta or cottage cheese; combine the cheese, the onion, a beaten egg, half a cup of breadcrumbs, and a handful of chopped mixed herbs (chervil, basil, dill, and mint, or any combination you like), salt, and pepper in a bowl. Form the mixture into small patties—about three inches wide—and fry over medium-high heat in the same skillet you used for the onion until brown, turning once and adding more olive oil if needed, about six minutes total.

93.

Deconstructed Raspberry Soufflés

Heat the oven to 400°F. Whip four egg whites and one teaspoon lemon zest until stiff peaks form. Toss two cups of fresh raspberries with two tablespoons brown sugar. Spoon raspberries into individual ramekins, top with a scoop of the whipped egg white, and sprinkle each with a teaspoon of slivered almonds if you like. Bake until tops are just golden, about eight minutes.

94.

Rose Water Whipped Cream with Honeydew

Just a little rose water works wonders.

Whip a cup of heavy cream with a few drops of rose water and a tablespoon of honey until thick. Cut a honeydew melon in half, scoop out the seeds, and slice into individual servings; serve each slice of melon with a dollop of the flavored whipped cream on top.

95.

Grilled Angel Food Cake
with Fruit Salsa

Obviously, homemade angel food is best, but store-bought can be good enough here.

Mix a cup of pitted halved cherries, a chopped mango, and two chopped peaches in a bowl with a quarter cup of sugar, a half teaspoon of cinnamon, juice from half a lemon, and the zest of the lemon. Smear slices of angel food cake with a little soft butter and grill each slice for about three minutes per side. Serve the fruit salsa over the angel food cake; garnish with chopped mint.

96.

Banana Ginger Granita

This takes only a couple of minutes to make,
but you do have to remember to freeze bananas in advance.

Put two fresh ripe frozen bananas, cut into two-inch pieces, in a food processor. Add two tablespoons of ginger ale or ginger beer and one-quarter cup crushed ice; pulse the mixture until smooth and serve, garnished with a grating of fresh ginger on top.

97.

Macerated Strawberries
with Mascarpone

Any orange-flavored liqueur works here.

In a bowl, mix together a quart of hulled, quartered strawberries, a couple of tablespoons of sugar, one-quarter cup Cointreau, freshly squeezed lemon juice, and lemon zest; let sit for five minutes or so. Serve in small bowls topped with a bit of mascarpone and good biscotti or any other crunchy cookie.

98.

Broiled Bananas

Keep an eye on these as they cook; they can go quickly from golden to overdone.

Heat the broiler and lightly butter a baking dish. Peel four bananas, cut them in half lengthwise, and arrange them on the dish. Dot the bananas with butter and sprinkle with brown sugar; broil about six inches from the flame until lightly browned, about five minutes. Serve hot, sprinkled with lemon or lime juice.

99.

Bittersweet Chocolate Crepes with Smashed Fruit

Crepes should be set and cooked through, but not crisp;
keep in mind that the first crepe almost never works.

In a blender, mix together one cup of flour, one-half cup cocoa powder, two eggs, one and one-half cups milk, one teaspoon vanilla extract, two tablespoons sugar, and two tablespoons melted butter; scrape down the sides until the mixture is smooth. Warm a bit of butter in a nonstick pan and ladle a thin coating of batter into the pan; swirl it around so it forms a thin layer on the bottom of the pan. Cook about 15 seconds or until the top looks dry; flip and cook 15 to 30 seconds more; repeat. Top with fresh smashed strawberries, raspberries, blueberries, or bananas.

100.

Chocolate Mousse

For a fruit mousse, substitute four ounces of pureed raspberries for the melted chocolate.

In a pan or in the microwave on low, melt two tablespoons of butter with four ounces of bittersweet or semisweet chocolate; set aside. Beat a cup of heavy cream with two tablespoons of sugar and a half teaspoon of vanilla until soft peaks form. Fold the whipped cream into the chocolate gently and stir until just combined; spoon the mousse into dishes, grate some chocolate on top if you like, and serve.

101.

Chocolate Hot Toddy

Serve with biscotti.

For each serving, melt one or two squares of semisweet chocolate in a cup and a half of milk, being sure not to bring the milk to a boil. Once the chocolate is melted, pour the milk into mugs and add a bit of dark rum or whiskey. Whipped cream is optional.

KITCHEN EXPRESS MENUS

Here are year-round ideas to help you use this book for every type of occasion. Obviously, you won't be able to pull together whole menus in 20 minutes, but you'll be amazed at how fast these meals come to the table, especially since many dishes can be made ahead and quickly reheated or served chilled or at room temperature.

WEEKNIGHT DINNER PARTY			
SUMMER	**FALL**	**WINTER**	**SPRING**
Gazpacho (page 31)	In-Shell Clam Chowder (page 71)	White Salad (page 125)	Snap Peas with Walnuts and Roquefort (page 175)
A Very Good Burger (page 58)		Mini Cannelloni (page 131)	
	Grilled Lamb Steak and White Bean Mash (page 102)	Garlic bread	Cajun-Style Salmon (page 178)
Assorted buns and trimmings bar		Lemon Mascarpone Mousse (page 153)	White rice
Blueberry Ricotta Cheesecakes (page 63)	Broiled Brussels Sprouts with Hazelnuts (page 82)		Green salad
	Dessert French Toast (page 111)		Grilled Angel Food Cake with Fruit Salsa (page 199)

BETTER-THAN-CHINESE-TAKEOUT			
SUMMER	**FALL**	**WINTER**	**SPRING**
Soba Noodles and Cucumber with Dipping Sauce (page 36)	Egg Drop Soup (page 72)	Squid Salad with Red Peppers and Cilantro (page 125)	Chive Salad (page 167)
	Sesame-Glazed Grilled Chicken (page 96)		Garlic-Ginger Shrimp (over Chinese egg noodles or white rice) (page 180)
Black and Blue Tuna (page 47)	Steamed white or brown rice	Crisp Tofu and Asian Greens with Peanut Sauce (page 131)	
Ginger-Lemon "Ice Cream" (page 64)	Apple Cider and White Wine Slushy (page 109)	White rice or rice noodles	Banana Ginger Granita (page 199)
		Grapefruit 'n' Cream Shake (page 153)	

ROMANTIC SUPPER			
SUMMER	**FALL**	**WINTER**	**SPRING**
Arugula with Balsamic Strawberries and Goat Cheese (page 38)	Endive and Warm Pear Salad with Stilton (page 76)	Avocado, Citrus, and Radicchio Salad (page 125)	Asparagus Leek Soup (page 163)
Grilled Lamb Chops with Summer Fruit (page 60)	Lavender-Thyme Braised Chicken (page 94)	Steak au Poivre (page 144)	Seared Scallops with White Wine and Chile (page 181)
		Potato Cumin Curry (page 132)	Crisp Fennel Gratin (page 175)
Frozen Hot Chocolate (page 64)	Pasta with Balsamic Onions (page 104)		
		Nutella Fondue (page 155)	
	Dark Chocolate Raspberry Pudding (page 110)		Bittersweet Chocolate Crepes with Smashed Fruit (page 200)

KIDS' NIGHT			
SUMMER	**FALL**	**WINTER**	**SPRING**
Grilled Chicken Kebabs (page 53)	Stir-Fried Mixed Vegetables with Ginger (page 85)	Meatball Subs (page 128)	Beef and Corn Tacos (page 189)
		Green Salad	
Pasta with Cherry Tomatoes (page 61)	Pasta Gratinée (page 108)	Chocolate Chip Pancakes (page 156)	Lettuce, tomato, guacamole, and all the trimmings
Ice Cream Sandwich (page 66)	Chocolate Panini (page 111)		Broiled Bananas (page 200)

ROOM-TEMPERATURE BUFFET			
SUMMER	**FALL**	**WINTER**	**SPRING**
Feta and Water-melon Salad (page 38)	Greek-Style Eggplant Salad (page 77)	Leek, Sun-Dried Tomato, and Goat Cheese Frittata (page 117)	Carrot and Cous-cous Salad (page 167)
	White Bean Toasts (page 79)		Lebanese Potato Salad (page 169)
Summertime Shrimp Salad (page 35)			
Pasta Salad with Beans and Herbs (page 61)	Flatbread Pizza with Figs, Goat Cheese, and Balsamic (page 83)	Date, Bacon, and Bean Salad (tossed with greens) (page 123)	Shrimp with Aspara-gus, Dill, and Spice (page 180)
Balsamic Beef, Radic-chio, and Romaine (page 45)	Seared Tuna with Capers and Toma-toes (page 90)	Scallop and Citrus Salad (page 124)	Spicy Pork Salad (page 169)
		Banderilla Pasta (page 148)	
			Deconstructed Raspberry Soufflés (page 198)
Fresh Fruit Gratin (page 65)	Sweet Couscous with Dried Fruit (page 112)	Almond Tart (page 155)	

FINGER-FOOD COCKTAIL PARTY			
SUMMER	**FALL**	**WINTER**	**SPRING**
Deviled Eggs with Crab (page 30)	Figs in a Blanket (page 80)	Eggs 'n' Capers (page 116) served on whole grain toast points	Carne Cruda on toasted baguette (page 190)
	Sesame Shrimp Toasts (page 92)		
Summer Rolls with Barbecued Pork (page 39)			Seared Fish with Lettuce Leaves (page 176)
Sausage and Grape Bruschetta (page 40)			
	Panini with Mushrooms and Fontina (cut into triangles) (page 80)	Shrimp with Black Bean Sauce (to eat with toothpicks) (page 133)	Mark's Famous Spicy Shrimp (served with toothpicks) (page 180)
Duck Wraps with Plums (page 39)	Turkey and Pear Wrap with Curry Aioli (page 81)	Scallion-Stuffed Beef Rolls (page 145)	
			Chicken Satay with Peanut Sauce (page 187)
Shrimp-Tomato-Arugula Wraps (page 41)	West Indian Pork Kebabs (page 99)	Fondue (page 129)	
		Simplest Chicken Kebabs (page 136)	Herbed Fresh Cheese Patties (made bite-size and served with toothpicks) (page 198)

PICNIC OR ROAD TRIP			
SUMMER	FALL	WINTER	SPRING
A thermos of chilled Charred Tomato Bisque (page 33)	Eggplant, Kalamata, Goat Cheese, and Dried Tomato Sandwich (page 81)	A thermos of Mixed Vegetable Soup (page 118)	Minted Pea and Prosciutto Sandwich (page 171)
Tuna Tabouleh (page 34)		White Bean and Salmon Sandwich (page 127)	Kettle-fried potato chips
Pita bread, olives, and feta cheese	Zucchini and Garlic Fusilli with Pistachios (served cold or at room temperature) (page 108)		Macerated Strawberries with Mascarpone (page 199)
		Candied Citrus Rinds (page 153)	
Peach Lemon "Cheesecake" (page 65)			
	Pound Cake with Mascarpone and Marmalade (page 110)		

HOLIDAY BLOWOUT			
SUMMER	**FALL**	**WINTER**	**SPRING**
Melon Soup with Pancetta (page 32)	Gruyère Apple Grilled Cheese (cut into triangles) (page 80)	Wild Mushroom Crostini (page 128)	Tuna and Bean Salad (served with crackers and olives) (page 170)
Avocado Crab Salad with Mixed Herb Salad (page 37)		Shrimp Bisque (page 121)	
	Cream of Turnip Soup (page 74)		Classic Caesar Salad (page 165)
		Pasta with Bacon and Breadcrumbs (page 151)	
Grilled Steaks with Rosemary Plums (page 57)	Seared Scallops with Almonds (page 91)		Spring Lamb (page 192)
Baked potatoes with butter	Fried Endive with Butter and Lemon Sauce (page 86)	Turkey Cutlets with Walnuts and Sage (and pureed apples) (page 142)	Cheesy Semolina with Asparagus (page 197)
			Chocolate Mousse (page 201)
Apricot Cream Upside-Down Pie (page 64)			
	Caramel Fondue (page 112)	Warm Milk Toast (page 152)	

WEEKEND BRUNCH			
SUMMER	FALL	WINTER	SPRING
Mexican Dry-Corn Salad (page 35)	Endive and Warm Pear Salad with Stilton (page 76)	Spinach Salad with Feta and Nutmeg (page 126)	Chilled Cucumber and Dill Soup (page 163)
Migas (page 33)			
Sour cream and assorted salsas	Mediterranean Poached Eggs (page 69)	Bacon, Eggs, and Grits (page 116)	Hangtown Fry (page 160)
			Buttered rye toast
		Biscuits with butter and honey	
Blackberries with Champagne and Tarragon (page 65)	Pumpkin Crème Brûlee (page 109)		Rose Water Whipped Cream with Honeydew (page 198)
		Orange Fool (page 154)	

OVEN TEMPERATURE EQUIVALENCIES

DESCRIPTION	°FAHRENHEIT	°CELSIUS
Cool	200	90
Very slow	250	120
Slow	300–325	150–160
Moderately slow	325–350	160–180
Moderate	350–375	180–190
Moderately hot	375–400	190–200
Hot	400–450	200–230
Very hot	450–500	230–260

ACKNOWLEDGMENTS

Sometime in early summer 2007 I had a conversation with Pete Wells, the *Times*'s Dining editor, which resulted in my writing "101 Summer Express Meals." Neither of us precisely remembers whose idea this was; as is often the case, it was a product of a good discussion, and I certainly won't take full credit for it.

The idea was to produce short, simple, inspiring ideas that would take ten minutes or less to make. Though the ten-minute rule proved difficult to maintain, the story was among the most popular in the paper that year, and remains among the most e-mailed of all time.

I won't take full credit for that, either. For the original article, I asked for ideas from anyone who would give them. This group included Dining colleagues Pat Gurosky, Nick Fox, Trish Hall, Julia Moskin, Pete of course, and Nicki Kalish, who also designed the paper's layout of the original story.

Nor was the idea of building on the concept to make a book mine; credit for that goes to my longtime agent and friend Angela Miller and my editor at Simon & Schuster, Sydny Miner. Others at Simon and Schuster I'd like to thank are David Rosenthal, Michelle Rorke, Alexis Welby and Jessica Abell, Mara Lurie, Michael Accordino, and Linda Dingler.

My colleagues Kerri Conan and Suzanne Lenzer worked hard on *Kitchen Express,* and they both know the depth of my gratitude. Stacey Ornstein helped with original research.

And Kelly Doe not only tweaked the design but lent moral support.

Mark Bittman
New York, Spring 2009

INDEX

aioli, curried, turkey and pear wrap with, 81

almonds, 11
    chicken with spinach and, 186
    chickpea soup with saffron and, 118
    seared scallops with, 91
    tart, 155

anchovies, 12
    banderilla pasta, 148
    classic Caesar salad, 165
    egg sandwich, 172
    pasta with breadcrumbs and, 193
    pasta with tomato tapenade, 149
    -tuna sandwich, 40

angel food cake, grilled, with fruit salsa, 199

appetizers (recipe list), 17

apple cider and white wine slushy, 109

apples, 13
    brown sugar, in microwave, 111
    chicken with sage and, 138
    -fennel slaw, pork tacos with, 99
    gruyère grilled cheese, 80
    à la mode, 112
    spinach salad with smoked trout and, 166

apricot:
    -braised lamb chops, 146
    cream upside-down pie, 64

arugula:
    with balsamic strawberries and goat cheese, 38
    pasta with garbanzo beans, sausage and, 151
    and prosciutto pasta, 195
    seared chicken rollups, 172
    -shrimp-tomato wraps, 41
    truffled, prosciutto salad, poached eggs with, 166

Asian greens and crisp tofu with peanut sauce, 131

Asian noodles, 11
    recipes to serve over (list), 25

asparagus:
    cheesy semolina with, 197
    leek soup, 163
    and sesame salad, 167
    shrimp with dill, spice and, 180

avocado, 12
    citrus, and radicchio salad, 125
    crab salad with mixed herb salad, 37
    dressing, for BLT salad, 168
    huevos rancheros, 70
    Mexican dry-corn salad, 35
    soup with crab, 32
    tuna with pineapple, cucumber and, 48

Aztec hot chocolate, 155

bacon, 12
    BLT salad, 168
    chicken with shallots, brandy and, 140
    date, and bean salad, 123
    eggs, and grits, 116
    Hangtown fry, 160
    pasta with breadcrumbs and, 151
    pear, and goat cheese sandwich, 126
    string beans with tomatoes and, 46
    warm cabbage salad with, 124
    -wrapped scallops, 52

balsamic beef, radicchio, and romaine, 45

balsamic onions, pasta with, 104

balsamic strawberries and goat cheese, arugula with, 38

banana ginger granita, 199

bananas, broiled, 200

banderilla pasta, 148

barbecue sauce, 10
    see also grilled foods
basil, 13
    -coconut sauce, spicy, chicken in, 136
    mayo, squid salad with, 35
    peanut sauce, grilled pork with, 57
    tomato, and goat cheese strata, 30
beans, 11
    braised cabbage with Spanish chorizo and, 130
    breakfast burritos, 70
    date, and bacon salad, 123
    four-bean salad, 36
    mixed, chili, 122
    mixed, soup or stew, 120
    pasta salad with herbs and, 61
    quick cassoulet, 122
    and tuna salad, 170
    see also white beans; specific beans
bean sprouts, spicy stir-fried, 175
bean threads, 11
beef:
    broiled steak with fennel and shallots, 189
    carne cruda, 190
    and corn tacos, 189
    fajita stir-fry, 145
    grilled steak with Gorgonzola sauce, 100
    grilled steaks with rosemary plums, 57
    Korean barbecued, 58
    meatball sub, 128
    miso burgers, 100
    and okra stir-fry, hot-and-sour, 59
    paillards with leeks and capers, 101
    radicchio, and romaine, balsamic, 45
    scallion-stuffed rolls, 145
    skirt steak with tomatillo salsa, 58
    steak au poivre, 144
    steak with butter and ginger, 190
    stir-fry with ginger noodles, 101
    stuffed burgers, 190
    tartar crostini, 127
    a very good burger, 58
    Vietnamese noodle soup with, 164

beer batter shrimp po'boy, 129
beets:
    and goat cheese salad, warm, 123
    raw, salad, 124
better-than-Chinese-takeout menu, 204
bittersweet chocolate crepes with smashed fruit, 200
black and blue tuna, 47
black beans, 11
    huevos rancheros, 70
    and mango salad, 34
    sauce, shrimp with, 133
    soup, 120
    tostada, 43
blackberries with Champagne and tarragon, 65
blackened salmon sandwich, 43
BLT salad, 168
blueberries:
    pancakes, 29
    ricotta cheesecakes, 63
blue cheese spread, grilled tomato sandwich with, 41
bok choy 'n' tofu, crisp, 87
brandy, chicken with bacon, shallots and, 140
bread, 12, 14
    chocolate panini, 111
    chorizo and manchego panini, 127
    dessert French toast, 111
    flatbread pizza with figs, goat cheese, and balsamic, 83
    Greek stuffed pita, 170
    Middle Eastern pizza, 173
    migas, 33
    panini with mushrooms and fontina, 80
    panzanella, 34
    sesame shrimp toasts, 92
    spicy escarole with croutons and eggs, 69
    warm milk toast, 152
    white bean toasts, 79
    zuppa di pane (soup), 119
breadcrumbs, 11
    pasta with anchovies and, 193
    pasta with bacon and, 151
    seared cauliflower with olives and, 82

breakfast:

    burritos, 70

    recipe list, 18–19

broccoli, 13

    poached tofu with, 63

broccoli rabe:

    and couscous, 176

    garlicky, with pancetta and pine nuts, 85

    and garlic soup, 74

    stuffed pork chops with, 144

broiled foods, 7-8

    bananas, 200

    Brussels sprouts with hazelnuts, 82

    eggplant, with miso-walnut vinaigrette, 39

    squid, 134

    steak with fennel and shallots, 189

    see also grilled foods

brown-bag lunches (list), 18

brown sugar apple in microwave, 111

brunch:

    baked eggs, 71

    menu, 209

    recipe list, 18–19

bruschetta, sausage and grape, 40

Brussels sprouts, 13

    broiled, with hazelnuts, 82

    shredded, grilled pork with, 98

bulgur, 10

    tuna tabouleh, 34

burritos, breakfast, 70

butter, 13

    and lemon sauce, fried endive with, 86

    Parmesan, and sage, linguine with, 149

    spicy lime, pan-seared fish with, 91

    steak with ginger and, 190

butter beans with prosciutto and mushrooms, 84

butternut squash–coconut soup, curried, 73

cabbage, 13

    braised, with Spanish chorizo and beans, 130

    and kielbasa sandwich, 128

    napa, stir-fried shrimp with chestnuts and, 90

pasta gratinée, 108

    and sausage, 98

    taco slaw, 44

    warm salad with bacon, 124

    white salad, 125

Caesar salad, classic, 165

Cajun-style salmon, 178

calf's liver, seared, with celery, 146

candied citrus rinds, 153

cannellini, 11

    date, bacon, and bean salad, 123

    tuna and bean salad, 170

    see also beans, white beans

cannelloni, mini, 131

capers, 10

    beef paillards with leeks and, 101

    'n' eggs, 116

    seared tuna with tomatoes and, 90

Caprese sandwich, caramelized, 41

caramel fondue, 112

caramelized grilled pork, Vietnamese, 188

caramelized pears with mascarpone, 109

carbonara, pasta, 194

carne cruda, 190

carrots, 13

    -chile-lime relish, grilled fish sandwich with, 42

    and couscous salad, 167

    and egg cake with soy, 70

cassoulet, quick, 122

cauliflower, 13

    seared, with olives and breadcrumbs, 82

    soup, 117

    white salad, 125

celery, 13

    seared calf's liver with, 146

celery root, braised pork chops with, 143

cellophane noodles:

    mussels with green curry and, 182

    with shrimp and papaya, 62

ceviche, scallop and peach, 49

Champagne, blackberries with tarragon and, 65

charred tomato bisque, 33

cheese, 13
    breakfast burritos, 70
    "burger," 172
    cheesy corn bread dumplings, 105
    cheesy semolina with asparagus, 197
    crisp fennel gratin, 175
    fondue, 129
    fresh, herbed patties, 198
    grilled, gruyère apple, 80
    pasta gratinée, 108
    saag paneer, 174
    stuffed burgers, 190
    see also specific types
cheesecakes:
    blueberry ricotta, 63
    peach lemon, 65
    quick lemon upside-down, 110
cherries:
    dried, pasta with herbed ricotta and, 104
    matzo brei with, 30
chervil, fried eggs with lemon and, 159
chestnuts and napa cabbage, stir-fried shrimp with, 90
chicken:
    with almonds and spinach, 186
    with apples and sage, 138
    with bacon, shallots, and brandy, 140
    braised, with olives and raisins, 93
    with chilaquiles and green salsa, 182
    with Chinese long beans and lemongrass, 54
    with coconut and lime, 187
    coconut-orange, 140
    coq au vin, 138
    curried salad sandwich, 171
    curry in a hurry, 95
    curry with raisins, 137
    with green olives, 185
    grilled, with prosciutto and figs, 95
    grilled kebabs, 53
    grilled lemon-tarragon, 52
    honey fried, 141
    honey-orange, 138
    jerk, 54

    lavender-thyme braised, 94
    and lemongrass soup, 161
    lemon Parmesan, 186
    lettuce wraps, 47
    and lime soup, 162
    maple-ginger glazed, with pecans, 139
    Mediterranean, 183
    Moroccan spiced, with yogurt sauce, 188
    paillards with endive and radicchio, 53
    pan-fried herbed, 185
    panko, with grapefruit-honey sauce, 184
    paprikash, 137
    pasta with frisée, Stilton and, 150
    piccata, 141
    poached in port, 141
    "potpie" salad sandwich, 171
    puttanesca, 96
    satay with peanut sauce, 187
    seared, arugula rollups, 172
    sesame-glazed grilled, 96
    simplest kebabs, 136
    spiced, with mango salsa, 55
    spicy, with lemongrass and lime, 184
    in spicy basil-coconut sauce, 136
    spicy tacos with chipotle cream, 55
    stir-fried, with nuts, 93
    with sweet-and-sour sherry sauce, 94
    tandoori, 183
    teriyaki skewers, 96
chicken livers with broad noodles, 139
chickpeas, 11
    burgers, 173
    hummus with pita, 78
    migas, 33
    pasta with sausage, arugula and, 151
    soup with saffron and almonds, 118
    tomato soup with greens and, 73
    and zucchini tagine, 120
chilaquiles, 159
    chicken with green salsa and, 182
chiles, 12
    -lime-carrot relish, grilled fish sandwich with, 42

seared scallops with white wine and, 181

    sweet potato soup, 74

chili, mixed bean, 122

chili powder, 12

Chinese egg noodles, dried, 11

Chinese long beans, chicken with lemongrass and, 54

chipotle cream, spicy chicken tacos with, 55

chives, 13

    orzo "risotto" with, 193

    salad, 167

chocolate, 11

    bittersweet, crepes with smashed fruit, 200

    chip pancakes, 156

    dark, raspberry pudding, 110

    drizzle, whipped grapefruit cream with, 154

    frozen hot, 64

    hot, Aztec, 155

    hot toddy, 201

    mousse, 201

    Nutella fondue, 155

    panini, 111

chorizo:

    and egg rollup, 129

    and manchego panini, 127

    Spanish, braised cabbage with beans and, 130

    Spanish, northern beans with, 87

    zucchini with tomatoes and, 46

chutney, raw pineapple, grilled fish with, 50

cilantro, 13

    lemony red lentil soup with, 72

    pesto, rice noodles with, 196

    shrimp with garlic, lime and, 51

    squid salad with red peppers and, 125

cinnamon, 12

citrus:

    avocado, and radicchio salad, 125

    -braised fish, 135

    candied rinds, 153

    and scallop salad, 124

    -soy glaze, crisp fish with wilted cress and, 179

clams:

    in-shell, chowder, 71

    stir-fried corn and, 52

cocoa powder, 11

coconut, 11

    -basil sauce, spicy, chicken in, 136

    -butternut squash soup, curried, 73

    chicken with lime and, 187

    curry sauce, salmon and sweet potato with, 89

    -orange chicken, 140

    toasted, shrimp with, 46

condiments, 10

cooking oils, 7, 10

coq au vin, 138

coriander, 12

corn:

    and beef tacos, 189

    dry, Mexican salad, 35

    stir-fried clams and, 52

    warm salad with ham, 37

corn bread cheesy dumplings, 105

cornmeal, 11

couscous, 10

    and broccoli rabe, 176

    and carrot salad, 167

    Moroccan lamb chops with, 103

    scallop stew with, 135

    seafood, 134

    sweet, with dried fruit, 112

crab:

    avocado salad with mixed herb salad, 37

    avocado soup with, 32

    cake burger, 51

    deviled eggs with, 30

    lettuce wraps, 47

    Vietnamese rice noodle salad with, 126

crackers, 11

cranberry-rosemary reduction, lamb chops with, 102

cream, 13

    'n' grapefruit shake, 153

    rose water whipped, with honeydew, 198

    whipped, grapefruit with chocolate frizzle, 154

cream of turnip soup, 74

crème brûlée, pumpkin, 109

crepes:

  bittersweet chocolate, with smashed fruit, 200

  Japanese egg, 116

cress, wilted, crisp fish with citrus-soy glaze and, 179

crostini:

  beef tartar, 127

  wild mushroom, 128

croutons, 11

  spicy escarole with eggs and, 69

cucumber:

  and dill soup, chilled, 163

  and soba noodles with dipping sauce, 36

  tuna with pineapple, avocado and, 48

cumin, 12

  potato curry, 132

  seared fish with lemon and, 133

currants, pasta with spinach, pine nuts and, 106

curries:

  chicken in a hurry, 95

  chicken salad sandwich, 171

  chicken with raisins, 137

  coconut—butternut squash soup, 73

  green, mussels with cellophane noodles and, 182

  potato cumin, 132

  salmon and sweet potato with coconut curry sauce, 89

  turkey and pear wrap with curried aioli, 81

curry powder, 12

date, bacon, and bean salad, 123

deconstructed raspberry soufflés, 198

desserts:

  almond tart, 155

  apple cider and white wine slushy, 109

  apples à la mode, 112

  apricot cream upside-down pie, 64

  Aztec hot chocolate, 155

  banana ginger granita, 199

  bittersweet chocolate crepes with smashed fruit, 200

  blackberries with Champagne and tarragon, 65

  blueberry ricotta cheesecakes, 63

  broiled bananas, 200

  brown sugar apple in the microwave, 111

  candied citrus rinds, 153

  caramel fondue, 112

  caramelized pears with mascarpone, 109

  chocolate chip pancakes, 156

  chocolate hot toddy, 201

  chocolate mousse, 201

  chocolate panini, 111

  dark chocolate raspberry pudding, 110

  deconstructed raspberry soufflés, 198

  French toast, 111

  fresh fruit gratin, 65

  frozen hot chocolate, 64

  ginger-lemon "ice cream," 64

  grapefruit 'n' cream shake, 153

  grilled angel food cake with fruit salsa, 199

  ice cream sandwich, 66

  lemon mascarpone mousse, 153

  macerated strawberries with mascarpone, 199

  Nutella fondue, 155

  orange fool, 154

  peach lemon "cheesecake," 65

  pound cake with mascarpone and marmalade, 110

  pumpkin crème brûlee, 109

  quick lemon upside-down cheesecake, 110

  quick summer fruit ice cream, 66

  recipe list, 19

  rose water whipped cream with honeydew, 198

  sweet couscous with dried fruit, 112

  warm milk toast, 152

  whipped grapefruit cream with chocolate drizzle, 154

deviled eggs with crab, 30

dill, 12

  and cucumber soup, chilled, 163

  shrimp with asparagus, spice and, 180

  and zucchini soup, 31

do-ahead recipes (list), 23

duck wraps with plums, 39

dumplings, cheesy corn bread, 105

easiest of the easiest (list), 21

edamame pesto, fish with, 178

eggplant, 13
    broiled, with miso-walnut vinaigrette, 39
    Greek-style salad, 77
    honey, microwaved, 44
    kalamata, goat cheese, and dried tomato sandwich,
      81
    rolls, 87
    stir-fry, 86
eggs, 13
    anchovy sandwich, 172
    bacon, and grits, 116
    bhona, 160
    breakfast burritos, 70
    brunch baked, 71
    and carrot cake with soy, 70
    cheese "burger," 172
    chilaquiles, 159
    and chorizo rollup, 129
    deviled, with crab, 30
    egg drop soup, 72
    fried, pasta with, 107
    fried, with lemon and chervil, 159
    Hangtown fry, 160
    in a hole with 'shrooms, 115
    huevos rancheros, 70
    Japanese crepes, 116
    leek, sun-dried tomato and goat cheese frittata,
      117
    Mediterranean poached, 69
    mixed herb omelet, 160
    'n' capers, 116
    pancetta and spinach frittata, 115
    pasta carbonara, 194
    poached, and truffled arugula prosciutto salad, 166
    poached, soup with greens and, 163
    -prosciutto sandwich, 130
    salad lyonnaise, 77
    spicy escarole with croutons and, 69
    Vietnamese noodle soup with beef, 164
endive:
    fried, with butter and lemon sauce, 86
    grilled chicken paillards with radicchio and, 53

    and warm pear salad with Stilton, 76
    white salad, 125
escarole:
    fennel, and orange salad, seared scallops with, 168
    spicy, with croutons and eggs, 69

fajita stir-fry, beef, 145
fast fish soup, 164
fennel:
    -apple slaw, pork tacos with, 99
    broiled steak with shallots and, 189
    crisp gratin, 175
    escarole, and orange salad, seared scallops with, 168
    -orange braised pork, 97
    seared fish with orange and, 178
    tuna sandwich with tarragon and, 79
feta:
    spinach salad with nutmeg and, 126
    and watermelon salad, 38
figs:
    in a blanket, 80
    flatbread pizza with goat cheese, balsamic and, 83
    grilled chicken with prosciutto and, 95
finger food:
    cocktail party menu, 206
    recipe list, 20
fish, 13
    baked, with oregano, lemon, and olives, 89
    braised, with cherry tomatoes, 50
    braised, with zucchini, 88
    braised in lemon with tomatoes and red peppers,
      177
    canned, 12
    citrus-braised, 135
    crisp, with citrus-soy glaze and wilted cress, 179
    with edamame pesto, 178
    fast soup, 164
    grilled, with peach and tomato salad, 48
    grilled, with raw pineapple chutney, 50
    grilled, with spinach and tomatoes, 49
    grilled kebabs, 48
    grilled sandwich with chile-lime-carrot relish, 42

fish (cont.)
   lettuce-wrapped, 132
   pan-seared, with spicy lime butter, 91
   prosciutto-wrapped, with wilted greens, 177
   seared, with cumin and lemon, 133
   seared, with fennel and orange, 178
   seared, with lettuce leaves, 176
   smoke 'n' spice soup, 32
   in spicy soy sauce, 176
   tacos, 40
   with Thai "pesto," 179
   walnut-coated, 88
fish sauce, Thai (nam pla), 10
five-spice lobster sandwich, 43
flatbread pizza with figs, goat cheese, and balsamic, 83
fleur de sel, 12
flour, 11
fondue, 129
   caramel, 112
   Nutella, 155
fontina, panini with mushrooms and, 80
fool, orange, 154
four-bean salad, 36
French toast, dessert, 111
frisée, pasta with chicken, Stilton and, 150
frittata:
   leek, sun-dried tomato, and goat cheese, 117
   pancetta and spinach, 115
frozen hot chocolate, 64
fruit, 13
   dried, 11
   dried, sweet couscous with, 112
   fresh, gratin, 65
   frozen, 14
   salsa, grilled angel food cake with, 199
   seasonal, 12
   smashed, bittersweet chocolate crepes with, 200
   summer, grilled lamb chops with, 60
   summer, quick ice cream, 66
   summertime shrimp salad, 35
   see also specific fruits
fusilli, zucchini and garlic, with pistachios, 108

garbanzo beans, pasta with sausage, arugula and, 151
garlic, 11
   and broccoli rabe soup, 74
   garlicky rabe with pancetta and pine nuts, 85
   -ginger shrimp, 180
   mussels in white wine and, 133
   shrimp with cilantro, lime and, 51
   and zucchini fusilli with pistachios, 108
gazpacho, 31
ginger, 11
   banana granita, 199
   -garlic shrimp, 180
   -lemon "ice cream," 64
   -maple glazed chicken with pecans, 139
   noodles, beef stir-fry with, 101
   steak with butter and, 190
   stir-fried mixed vegetables with, 85
glass noodles, 11
goat cheese:
   arugula with balsamic strawberries and, 38
   and beet salad, warm, 123
   eggplant, kalamata, and dried tomato sandwich, 81
   flatbread pizza with figs, balsamic and, 83
   leek, and sun-dried tomato frittata, 117
   pear, and bacon sandwich, 126
   salad, 33
   spinach salad with oranges and, 76
   tomato, and basil strata, 30
Gorgonzola sauce, grilled steak with, 100
grains, quick-cooking, 10
granita, banana ginger, 199
grape and sausage bruschetta, 40
grapefruit, 13
   -honey sauce, panko chicken with, 184
   'n' cream shake, 153
   whipped cream with chocolate drizzle, 154
grapeseed oil, 7, 10
gravy, redeye, ham steak with, 100
Greek stuffed pita bread, 170
Greek-style eggplant salad, 77
greens:
   Asian, and crisp tofu with peanut sauce, 131

soup with poached eggs and, 163

tomato soup with chickpeas and, 73

wilted, prosciutto-wrapped fish with, 177

see also salads; specific greens

green tea broth, udon noodles with, 161

grilled foods:

angel food cake with fruit salsa, 199

charred tomato bisque, 33

cheese, gruyère apple, 80

chicken kebabs, 53

chicken paillards with endive and radicchio, 53

chicken tandoori, 183

chicken with prosciutto and figs, 95

eggplant with miso-walnut vinaigrette, 39

fish, with peach and tomato salad, 48

fish, with raw pineapple chutney, 50

fish, with spinach and tomatoes, 49

fish kebabs, 48

fish sandwich with chile-lime-carrot relish, 42

Korean barbecued beef, 58

lamb chops with lemony yogurt sauce, 59

lamb chops with summer fruit, 60

lamb steak and white bean mash, 102

lemon-tarragon chicken, 52

Mark's famous spicy shrimp, 180

pineapple, pork paillards with, 56

pork skewers with Worcestershire, 56

pork with basil peanut sauce, 57

pork with shredded Brussels sprouts, 98

sardines with summer squash, 49

sesame-glazed chicken, 96

skirt steak with tomatillo salsa, 58

spicy pork with peach marmalade, 56

steaks with rosemary plums, 57

steak with Gorgonzola sauce, 100

tomato sandwich with blue cheese spread, 41

vegetables with quinoa, 47

Vietnamese caramelized pork, 188

watermelon and shrimp skewers, 50

see also broiled foods

grits, bacon, and eggs, 116

gruyère apple grilled cheese, 80

ham, 13

steak with redeye gravy, 100

warm corn salad with, 37

white bean stew, 119

see also prosciutto

Hangtown fry, 160

hazelnuts, 11

broiled Brussels sprouts with, 82

herbs, 12, 13

fresh cheese patties, 198

mixed, omelet, 160

mixed, avocado crab salad with, 37

pan-fried chicken, 185

pasta salad with beans and, 61

hoisin sauce, 10

eggplant stir-fry, 86

holiday blowout menu, 208

honey:

eggplant, microwaved, 44

fried chicken, 141

-grapefruit sauce, panko chicken with, 184

-orange chicken, 138

honeydew, rose water whipped cream with, 198

hot-and-sour beef and okra stir-fry, 59

hot chocolate:

Aztec, 155

frozen, 64

hot pepper sauce, 10

hot toddy, chocolate, 201

huevos rancheros, 70

hummus:

chickpea burgers, 173

with pita, 78

ice cream:

apples à la mode, 112

ginger-lemon "ice cream," 64

quick summer fruit, 66

sandwich, 66

Indian-style lamb kebabs, 147

ingredients:

on the counter, 12

ingredients (*cont.*)
    in the cupboard, 9–12
    in the freezer, 14
    in the fridge, 12–13
    in the pantry, 9–14
    substitutions, 8, 15
in-shell clam chowder, 71
Italian tostada, 173

jambalaya, pasta, 148
Japanese egg crepes, 116
jerk chicken, 54

kalamata, eggplant, goat cheese, and dried tomato
    sandwich, 81
kale and prosciutto sandwich, 79
kasha, 10
kebabs:
    chicken satay with peanut sauce, 187
    chicken tandoori, 183
    chicken teriyaki skewers, 96
    grilled chicken, 53
    grilled fish, 48
    grilled pork skewers with Worcestershire, 56
    grilled watermelon and shrimp skewers, 50
    Indian-style lamb, 147
    shrimp, scallop, and cherry tomato, 51
    simplest chicken, 136
    West Indian pork, 99
ketchup, 10
ketchup-braised tofu with veggies, 174
kids' night menu, 205
kielbasa:
    and cabbage sandwich, 128
    sweet sauerkraut with, 142
Korean barbecued beef, 58

lamb:
    apricot-braised chops, 146
    braised chops with prunes, 103
    chops with cranberry-rosemary reduction, 102
    grilled chops with lemony yogurt sauce, 59

grilled chops with summer fruit, 60
grilled steak, and white bean mash, 102
"gyro," 191
Indian-style kebabs, 147
kibbe, 191
Middle Eastern pizza, 173
Moroccan chops with couscous, 103
red wine–braised chops, 147
spring, 192
lavender-thyme braised chicken, 94
Lebanese potato salad, 169
leeks:
    asparagus soup, 163
    beef paillards with capers and, 101
    sun-dried tomato, and goat cheese frittata, 117
lemongrass:
    chicken with Chinese long beans and, 54
    and chicken soup, 161
    shrimp with, 134
    spicy chicken with lime and, 184
lemons, 13
    baked fish with oregano, olives and, 89
    and butter sauce, fried endive with, 86
    fish braised in, with tomatoes and red peppers, 177
    fried eggs with chervil and, 159
    -ginger "ice cream," 64
    lemony red lentil soup with cilantro, 72
    lemony yogurt sauce, grilled lamb chops with, 59
    mascarpone mousse, 153
    Parmesan chicken, 186
    peach "cheesecake," 65
    quick upside-down cheesecake, 110
    sauce, pasta with, 195
    seared fish with cumin and, 133
    -soy sauce, udon noodles with seafood and, 197
    -tarragon chicken, grilled, 52
lentils, 11
    red, lemony soup with cilantro, 72
    red, sausage with, 99
lettuce leaves, with seared fish, 176
lettuce-wrapped fish, 132
lettuce wraps, 47

lima bean stew, 121

limes, 13

    chicken with coconut and, 187

    and chicken soup, 162

    -chile-carrot relish, grilled fish sandwich with, 42

    shrimp with cilantro, garlic and, 51

    spicy butter, pan-seared fish with, 91

    spicy chicken with lemongrass and, 184

linguica and cabbage sandwich, 128

linguine:

    with butter, Parmesan, and sage, 149

    with pea sauce and prosciutto, 152

lobster sandwich, five-spice, 43

lyonnaise salad, 77

macerated strawberries with mascarpone, 199

manchego and chorizo panini, 127

mango:

    and black bean salad, 34

    salsa, spiced chicken with, 55

maple-ginger glazed chicken with pecans, 139

Mark's famous spicy shrimp, 180

mascarpone:

    caramelized pears with, 109

    lemon mousse, 153

    macerated strawberries with, 199

    pound cake with marmalade and, 110

matzo brei with cherries, 30

mayonnaise, 10

measurements, estimating, 3

meat, 13, 14

meatball sub, 128

Mediterranean chicken, 183

Mediterranean poached eggs, 69

melon:

    rose water whipped cream with honeydew, 198

    soup with pancetta, 32

menus:

    better-than-Chinese-takeout, 204

    finger-food cocktail party, 206

    holiday blowout, 208

    kids' night, 205

    picnic or road trip, 207

    romantic supper, 204

    room-temperature buffet, 205

    weekend brunch, 209

    weeknight dinner party, 203

Mexican dry-corn salad, 35

Middle Eastern pizza, 173

migas, 33

milk, 13

milk toast, warm, 152

mini cannelloni, 131

minted pea and prosciutto sandwich, 171

miso, 13

    burgers, 100

    soup with tofu, 162

    and udon noodle soup with fresh shiitake

        mushrooms, 75

    -walnut vinaigrette, broiled eggplant with, 39

Moroccan lamb chops with couscous, 103

Moroccan spiced chicken with yogurt sauce, 188

Moroccan tapenade, pasta with, 194

mozzarella, prosciutto, and peach salad, 37

muesli with raspberries, 29

mushrooms:

    butter beans with prosciutto and, 84

    egg in a hole with 'shrooms, 115

    fresh shiitake, udon noodle and miso soup with, 75

    Hangtown fry, 160

    and nori soup, 72

    panini with fontina and, 80

    pasta, 105

    wild, crostini, 128

mussels:

    with green curry and cellophane noodles, 182

    in tomato–white bean sauce, 92

    in white wine and garlic, 133

mustard, 10, 12

nam pla (Thai fish sauce), 10

napa cabbage, stir-fried shrimp with chestnuts and,

    90

niçoise, salad, 165

INDEX

noodles:
    Asian, 11
    broad, chicken livers with, 139
    cellophane, mussels with green curry and, 182
    cellophane, with shrimp and papaya, 62
    ginger, beef stir-fry with, 101
    recipes to serve over, 25
    rice, Vietnamese, salad with crab, 126
    rice, with cilantro pesto, 196
    seafood ramen, 75
    shrimp pad Thai, 196
    soba, and cucumber with dipping sauce, 36
    soba, spicy pork with, 107
    udon, and miso soup with fresh shiitake mushrooms, 75
    udon, with green tea broth, 161
    udon, with seafood and soy-lemon sauce, 197
    Vietnamese soup with beef, 164
nori and mushroom soup, 72
northern beans with Spanish chorizo, 87
Nutella fondue, 155
nutmeg, spinach salad with feta and, 126
nuts, 11
    stir-fried chicken with, 93
    see also specific nuts

oats, steel-cut, 10
okra and beef stir-fry, hot-and-sour, 59
olive oil, extra-virgin, 7, 10
olives, 13
    baked fish with oregano, lemon and, 89
    braised chicken with raisins and, 93
    green, chicken with, 185
    kalamata, eggplant, goat cheese, and dried tomato sandwich, 81
    seared cauliflower with breadcrumbs and, 82
    seared pork paillards with prunes and, 143
omelet, mixed herb, 160
onions, 11
    balsamic, pasta with, 104
oranges, 13
    -coconut chicken, 140

escarole, and fennel salad, seared scallops with, 168
    -fennel braised pork, 97
    fool, 154
    -honey chicken, 138
    seared fish with fennel and, 178
    spinach salad with goat cheese and, 76
oregano, 12, 13
    baked fish with lemon, olives and, 89
orzo "risotto" with chives, 193
oven temperature equivalencies, 210
oysters, Hangtown fry, 160

pad Thai, shrimp, 196
pancakes:
    blueberry, 29
    chocolate chip, 156
pancetta, 12
    garlicky rabe with pine nuts and, 85
    melon soup with, 32
    pasta carbonara, 194
    and spinach frittata, 115
    Swiss chard with white beans and, 45
panini:
    chocolate, 111
    chorizo and manchego, 127
    with mushrooms and fontina, 80
panko breadcrumbs, 11
    chicken with grapefruit-honey sauce, 184
panzanella, 34
papaya:
    cellophane noodles with shrimp and, 62
    green, salad, with shrimp, 170
paprikash, chicken, 137
Parmesan, 13
    lemon chicken, 186
    linguine with butter, sage and, 149
parsley, 13
pasta, 11
    with anchovies and breadcrumbs, 193
    arugula and prosciutto, 195
    with bacon and breadcrumbs, 151
    with balsamic onions, 104

banderilla, 148

carbonara, 194

with cherry tomatoes, 61

with chicken, frisée, and Stilton, 150

chicken livers with broad noodles, 139

with fried eggs, 107

with garbanzo beans, sausage, and arugula, 151

gratinée, 108

with herbed ricotta and dried cherries, 104

jambalaya, 148

with lemon sauce, 195

linguine with butter, Parmesan, and sage, 149

linguine with pea sauce and prosciutto, 152

with Moroccan tapenade, 194

mushroom, 105

penne with vodka sauce, 106

with puttanesca cruda, 63

recipes to toss with (list), 24

salad with beans and herbs, 61

and shrimp with pesto, 60

with spicy shellfish, 62

with spicy squid, 61

with spinach, currants, and pine nuts, 106

with tomato tapenade, 149

with walnut pesto, 150

zucchini and garlic fusilli with pistachios, 108

peaches:

lemon "cheesecake," 65

prosciutto, and mozzarella salad, 37

and scallop ceviche, 49

and tomato salad, grilled fish with, 48

peach marmalade, spicy grilled pork with, 56

peanut oil, 7, 10

peanuts, 11

peanut sauce:

basil, grilled pork with, 57

chicken satay with, 187

crisp tofu and Asian greens with, 131

peanuts; peanut butter, 11

chicken satay with peanut sauce, 187

crisp tofu and Asian greens with peanut sauce, 131

grilled pork with basil peanut sauce, 57

peanut soup, 117

pears:

bacon, and goat cheese sandwich, 126

caramelized, with mascarpone, 109

sweet sauerkraut with kielbasa, 142

and turkey wrap with curried aioli, 81

warm, and endive salad with Stilton, 76

peas:

minted, and prosciutto sandwich, 171

"potpie" chicken salad sandwich, 171

sauce, linguine with prosciutto and, 152

snap, with walnuts and Roquefort, 175

split, 11

pecans, maple-ginger glazed chicken with, 139

penne with vodka sauce, 106

Pepin, Jacques, 3

pepper, 12

peppers, red:

fish braised in lemon with tomatoes and, 177

squid salad with cilantro and, 125

tofu with pineapple and, 130

pesto:

cilantro, rice noodles with, 196

edamame, fish with, 178

fish with Thai "pesto," 179

shrimp and pasta with, 60

walnut, pasta with, 150

piccata, chicken, 141

picnic menu, 207

picnics:

best recipes (list), 22

menu, 207

pineapple, 13

grilled, pork paillards with, 56

raw, chutney, grilled fish with, 50

tofu with red peppers and, 130

tuna with cucumber, avocado and, 48

pine nuts:

garlicky rabe with pancetta and, 85

pasta with spinach, currants and, 106

pinto beans, 11

pistachios, zucchini and garlic fusilli with, 108

pita:

    Greek stuffed, 170

    hummus with, 78

    lamb "gyro," 191

pizza:

    flatbread, with figs, goat cheese, and balsamic, 83

    Middle Eastern, 173

plums:

    duck wraps with, 39

    rosemary, grilled steaks with, 57

pork:

    barbecued, summer rolls with, 39

    braised, with rosemary, 97

    braised chops with celery root, 143

    fennel-orange braised, 97

    grilled, with basil peanut sauce, 57

    grilled, with shredded Brussels sprouts, 98

    grilled skewers with Worcestershire, 56

    miso burgers, 100

    paillards with grilled pineapple, 56

    seared paillards with prunes and olives, 143

    spicy, with soba noodles, 107

    spicy grilled, with peach marmalade, 56

    spicy salad, 169

    stuffed chops with broccoli rabe, 144

    tacos with apple-fennel slaw, 99

    Vietnamese caramelized grilled, 188

    West Indian kebabs, 99

port, chicken poached in, 141

portobello burgers with tomato mayonnaise, 42

potatoes, 12

    cumin curry, 132

    in-shell clam chowder, 71

    Lebanese salad, 169

    pasta gratinée, 108

    and sausage, 142

potlucks (recipe list), 23

"potpie" chicken salad sandwich, 172

poultry, 13, 14; see also chicken; turkey

pound cake with mascarpone and marmalade, 110

prosciutto, 13

    and arugula pasta, 195

    butter beans with mushrooms and, 84

    -egg sandwich, 130

    grilled chicken with figs and, 95

    and kale sandwich, 79

    linguine with pea sauce and, 152

    and minted pea sandwich, 171

    peach, and mozzarella salad, 37

    truffled arugula salad, poached eggs and, 166

    -wrapped fish with wilted greens, 177

prunes:

    braised lamb chops with, 103

    seared pork paillards with olives and, 143

pumpkin crème brûlée, 109

pumpkin seeds, 11

puttanesca, chicken, 96

puttanesca cruda, pasta with, 63

quick cassoulet, 122

quick lemon upside-down cheesecake, 110

quick summer fruit ice cream, 66

quinoa, 10

    grilled vegetables with, 47

radicchio:

    avocado, and citrus salad, 125

    beef, and romaine, balsamic, 45

    grilled chicken paillards with endive and, 53

raisins:

    braised chicken with olives and, 93

    chicken curry with, 137

    spiced vegetables with, 84

    warm milk toast, 152

ramen, seafood, 75

raspberries:

    dark chocolate pudding, 110

    deconstructed soufflés, 198

    muesli with, 29

redeye gravy, ham steak with, 100

reheating, recipes for (list), 22–23

rice, 10

    recipes to serve over (list), 25

rice noodles:
> with cilantro pesto, 196
> Vietnamese, salad with crab, 126
rice sticks, 11
ricotta:
> blueberry cheesecakes, 63
> herbed, pasta with dried cherries and, 104
road trip menu, 207
romaine:
> beef, and radicchio, balsamic, 45
> seared scallops with, 123
romantic supper menu, 204
room-temperature buffet menu, 205
Roquefort, snap peas with walnuts and, 175
rosemary, 12, 13
> braised pork with, 97
> -cranberry reduction, lamb chops with, 102
> plums, grilled steaks with, 57
rose water whipped cream with honeydew, 198
roux, how to make, 148

saag paneer, 174
saffron, 12
> chickpea soup with almonds and, 118
sage, 13
> chicken with apples and, 138
> linguine with butter, Parmesan and, 149
> turkey cutlets with walnuts and, 142
salads:
> arugula with balsamic strawberries and goat cheese, 38
> asparagus and sesame, 167
> avocado, citrus, and radicchio, 125
> avocado crab with mixed herb, 37
> balsamic beef, radicchio, and romaine, 45
> black bean and mango, 34
> BLT, 168
> carrot and couscous, 167
> chive, 167
> classic Caesar, 165
> crisp tofu and Asian greens with peanut sauce, 131
> curried chicken, sandwich, 171

date, bacon, and bean, 123
endive and warm pear, with Stilton, 76
escarole, fennel, and orange salad, seared scallops with, 168
feta and watermelon, 38
four-bean, 36
goat cheese, 33
Greek stuffed pita bread, 170
Greek-style eggplant, 77
green papaya, with shrimp, 170
hummus with pita, 78
Lebanese potato, 169
lyonnaise, 77
Mexican dry-corn, 35
niçoise, 165
panzanella, 34
pasta with beans and herbs, 61
peach and tomato, grilled fish with, 48
pork tacos with apple-fennel slaw, 99
"potpie" chicken, sandwich, 171
prosciutto, peach, and mozzarella, 37
raw beet, 124
scallop and citrus, 124
scallop and peach ceviche, 49
seared scallops with romaine, 123
shrimp and cherry tomato, 38
spicy pork, 169
spinach, with feta and nutmeg, 126
spinach, with oranges and goat cheese, 76
spinach, with smoked trout and apples, 166
squid, with basil mayo, 35
squid, with red peppers and cilantro, 125
summertime shrimp, 35
Swiss chard with white beans and pancetta, 45
taco slaw, 44
tofu, 78
truffled arugula prosciutto, poached eggs and, 166
tuna and bean, 170
tuna tabouleh, 34
Vietnamese rice noodle, with crab, 126
warm beet and goat cheese, 123
warm cabbage with bacon, 124

INDEX

salads (*cont.*)
    warm corn, with ham, 37
    white, 125
salami and cabbage sandwich, 128
salmon, 12
    blackened, sandwich, 43
    Cajun-style, 178
    and sweet potato with coconut curry sauce, 89
    and white bean sandwich, 127
salsa, 10
    fruit, grilled angel food cake with, 199
    green, chicken with chilaquiles and, 182
    mango, spiced chicken with, 55
    tomatillo, grilled skirt steak with, 58
salt, 12
sandwiches:
    anchovy egg, 172
    beef tartar crostini, 127
    beer batter shrimp po'boy, 129
    blackened salmon, 43
    cabbage and kielbasa, 128
    caramelized caprese, 41
    cheese "burger," 172
    chickpea burgers, 173
    chorizo and egg rollup, 129
    chorizo and manchego panini, 127
    crab cake burger, 51
    curried chicken salad, 171
    duck wraps with plums, 39
    eggplant, kalamata, goat cheese, and dried tomato, 81
    fish tacos, 40
    five-spice lobster, 43
    Greek stuffed pita bread, 170
    grilled fish with chile-lime-carrot relish, 42
    grilled tomato with blue cheese spread, 41
    gruyère apple grilled cheese, 80
    hot (recipe list), 24
    ice cream, 66
    kale and prosciutto, 79
    lettuce wraps, 47
    meatball sub, 128
    minted pea and prosciutto, 171

miso burgers, 100
panini with mushrooms and fontina, 80
pear, bacon, and goat cheese, 126
portobello burgers with tomato mayonnaise, 42
"potpie" chicken salad, 171
prosciutto-egg, 130
sausage and grape bruschetta, 40
seared chicken arugula rollups, 172
shrimp-tomato-arugula wraps, 41
stuffed burgers, 190
summer rolls with barbecued pork, 39
tuna-anchovy, 40
tuna with fennel and tarragon, 79
tuna with pineapple, cucumber, and avocado, 48
turkey and pear wrap with curried aioli, 81
a very good burger, 58
white bean and salmon, 127
white bean toasts, 79
wild mushroom crostini, 128
sardines, 12
    grilled, with summer squash, 49
satay, chicken, with peanut sauce, 187
sauces, 10
    basil peanut, grilled pork with, 57
    black bean, shrimp with, 133
    butter, Parmesan, and sage, linguine with, 149
    butter and lemon, fried endive with, 86
    caramelized, Vietnamese grilled pork, 188
    carbonara, pasta, 194
    chipotle cream, spicy chicken tacos with, 55
    citrus-soy glaze, crisp fish with wilted cress and, 179
    coconut curry, salmon and sweet potato with, 89
    cranberry-rosemary reduction, lamb chops with, 102
    curried aioli, turkey and pear wrap with, 81
    dipping, for soba noodles and cucumber, 36
    Gorgonzola, grilled steak with, 100
    grapefruit-honey, panko chicken with, 184
    lemon, pasta with, 195
    lemony yogurt, grilled lamb chops with, 59
    Moroccan tapenade, pasta with, 194
    for pasta, 24
    pea, linguine with prosciutto and, 152

peach marmalade, spicy grilled pork with, 56

peanut, chicken satay with, 187

peanut, crisp tofu and Asian greens with, 131

piccata, chicken, 141

puttanesca, chicken, 96

puttanesca cruda, pasta with, 63

redeye gravy, ham steak with, 100

salad lyonnaise, 77

soy-lemon, udon noodles with seafood and, 197

spicy basil-coconut, chicken in, 136

spicy lime butter, pan-seared fish with, 91

spicy soy, fish in, 176

sweet-and-sour sherry, chicken with, 94

tomato tapenade, pasta with, 149

tomato–white bean, mussels in, 92

vodka, penne with, 106

yogurt, Moroccan spiced chicken with, 188

see also pesto; salsa

sauerkraut, sweet, with kielbasa, 142

sausage:

braised cabbage with Spanish chorizo and beans, 130

and cabbage, 98

and cabbage sandwich, 128

chorizo and manchego panini, 127

and grape bruschetta, 40

northern beans with Spanish chorizo, 87

pasta jambalaya, 148

pasta with garbanzo beans, arugula and, 151

and potatoes, 142

quick cassoulet, 122

with red lentils, 99

stuffed pork chops with broccoli rabe, 144

sweet sauerkraut with kielbasa, 142

zucchini with tomatoes and chorizo, 46

scallions:

scallops with sesame seeds and, 181

-stuffed beef rolls, 145

scallops:

bacon-wrapped, 52

and citrus salad, 124

and peach ceviche, 49

seared, with almonds, 91

seared, with escarole, fennel, and orange salad, 168

seared, with romaine, 123

seared, with white wine and chile, 181

with sesame seeds and scallions, 181

shrimp, and cherry tomato kebabs, 51

stew with couscous, 135

seafood:

couscous, 134

ramen, 75

udon noodles with soy-lemon sauce and, 197

see also fish; specific seafoods

seeds, 11

semolina, cheesy, with asparagus, 197

sesame:

and asparagus salad, 167

black and blue tuna, 47

-glazed grilled chicken, 96

shrimp toasts, 92

sesame oil, 10

sesame seeds, 11

scallops with scallions and, 181

shallots, 11

broiled steak with fennel and, 189

chicken with bacon, brandy and, 140

shellfish:

spicy, pasta with, 62

see also specific shellfish

sherry sauce, sweet-and-sour, chicken with, 94

sherry vinegar, 10

shiitake mushrooms, fresh, udon noodle and miso soup with, 75

shrimp:

with asparagus, dill, and spice, 180

beer batter po'boy, 129

bisque, 121

with black bean sauce, 133

cellophane noodles with papaya and, 62

and cherry tomato salad, 38

with cilantro, garlic, and lime, 51

garlic-ginger, 180

green papaya salad with, 170

with lemongrass, 134

shrimp (cont.)

    pad Thai, 196

    and pasta with pesto, 60

    scallop, and cherry tomato kebabs, 51

    sesame toasts, 92

    spicy, Mark's famous, 180

    stir-fried, with chestnuts and napa cabbage, 90

    summertime salad, 35

    with toasted coconut, 46

    -tomato-arugula wraps, 41

    and tomato soup, 31

    and watermelon skewers, grilled, 50

smoke 'n' spice fish soup, 32

soba noodles, 11

    and cucumber with dipping sauce, 36

    spicy pork with, 107

somen noodles, 11

soufflés, deconstructed raspberry, 198

soups:

    asparagus leek, 163

    avocado, with crab, 32

    black bean, 120

    broccoli rabe and garlic, 74

    cauliflower, 117

    charred tomato bisque, 33

    chickpea, with saffron and almonds, 118

    chile sweet potato, 74

    to chill, 25

    chilled cucumber and dill, 163

    cream of turnip, 74

    curried coconut–butternut squash, 73

    egg drop, 72

    fast fish, 164

    gazpacho, 31

    in-shell clam chowder, 71

    lemongrass-and-chicken, 161

    lemony red lentil, with cilantro, 72

    lime and chicken, 162

    melon, with pancetta, 32

    miso, with tofu, 162

    mixed bean, 120

    mixed vegetable, 118

    mushroom and nori, 72

    peanut, 117

    with poached eggs and greens, 163

    seafood ramen, 75

    shrimp and tomato, 31

    shrimp bisque, 121

    smoke 'n' spice fish, 32

    spinach and white bean, 162

    tomato, with chickpeas and greens, 73

    udon noodle and miso, with fresh shiitake mushrooms, 75

    udon noodles with green tea broth, 161

    Vietnamese noodle with beef, 164

    zucchini and dill, 31

    zuppa di pane (bread), 119

sour cream, 13

soy-lemon sauce, udon noodles with seafood and, 197

soy sauce, 10

    egg and carrot cake with, 70

    spicy, fish in, 176

Spanish chorizo:

    braised cabbage with beans and, 130

    northern beans with, 87

spiced chicken with mango salsa, 55

spiced vegetables with raisins, 84

spices, 12

spicy chicken tacos with chipotle cream, 55

spicy chicken with lemongrass and lime, 184

spicy escarole with croutons and eggs, 69

spicy grilled pork with peach marmalade, 56

spicy pork salad, 169

spicy pork with soba noodles, 107

spicy shrimp, Mark's famous, 180

spicy stir-fried bean sprouts, 175

spinach:

    brunch baked eggs, 71

    chicken with almonds and, 186

    grilled fish with tomatoes and, 49

    and pancetta frittata, 115

    pasta with currants, pine nuts and, 106

    saag paneer, 174

    salad with feta and nutmeg, 126

salad with oranges and goat cheese, 76
    salad with smoked trout and apples, 166
    and white bean soup, 162
spring lamb, 192
squash, 12, 13
    braised fish with zucchini, 88
    butternut,–coconut soup, curried, 73
    chickpea and zucchini tagine, 120
    summer, grilled sardines with, 49
    zucchini and dill soup, 31
    zucchini and garlic fusilli with pistachios, 108
    zucchini with tomatoes and chorizo, 46
squid:
    broiled, 134
    salad with basil mayo, 35
    salad with red peppers and cilantro, 125
    spicy, pasta with, 61
steak:
    au poivre, 144
    see also beef
stews:
    chicken paprikash, 137
    chickpea and zucchini tagine, 120
    lima bean, 121
    mixed bean, 120
    mixed bean chili, 122
    pasta jambalaya, 148
    quick cassoulet, 122
    scallop, with couscous, 135
    white bean, 119
Stilton:
    endive and warm pear salad with, 76
    pasta with chicken, frisée and, 150
stock, 10
strawberries:
    balsamic, arugula with goat cheese and, 38
    macerated, with mascarpone, 199
string beans, 13
    with bacon and tomatoes, 46
sub, meatball, 128
substitutions, 8, 15
summer rolls with barbecued pork, 39

sunflower seeds, 11
sweet-and-sour sherry sauce, chicken with, 94
sweet potatoes, 12
    chile soup, 74
    and salmon with coconut curry sauce, 89
Swiss chard with white beans and pancetta, 45

tabouleh, tuna, 34
tacos:
    beef and corn, 189
    fish, 40
    pork, with apple-fennel slaw, 99
    slaw, 44
    spicy chicken, with chipotle cream, 55
tagine, chickpea and zucchini, 120
tapenade:
    Moroccan, pasta with, 194
    tomato, pasta with, 149
tarragon, 12
    blackberries with Champagne and, 65
    -lemon chicken, grilled, 52
    tuna sandwich with fennel and, 79
tart, almond, 155
tea, green, broth, udon noodles with, 161
teriyaki chicken skewers, 96
Thai "pesto," fish with, 179
thyme, 12
    -lavender braised chicken, 94
tofu:
    crisp, and Asian greens with peanut sauce, 131
    ketchup-braised, with veggies, 174
    miso soup with, 162
    'n' bok choy, crisp, 87
    with pineapple and red peppers, 130
    poached, with broccoli, 63
    salad, 78
tomatillo salsa, grilled skirt steak with, 58
tomatoes:
    BLT salad, 168
    canned, 10
    charred bisque, 33
    cherry, and shrimp salad, 38

tomatoes (cont.)

    cherry, braised fish with, 50

    cherry, pasta with, 61

    cherry, shrimp, and scallop kebabs, 51

    dried, 11

    dried, eggplant, kalamata, and goat cheese sandwich,
      81

    fast fish soup, 164

    fish braised in lemon with red peppers and, 177

    gazpacho, 31

    goat cheese, and basil strata, 30

    grilled fish with spinach and, 49

    grilled sandwich with blue cheese spread, 41

    mayonnaise, portobello burgers with, 42

    panzanella, 34

    and peach salad, grilled fish with, 48

    scallop stew with couscous, 135

    seared tuna with capers and, 90

    -shrimp-arugula wraps, 41

    and shrimp soup, 31

    soup with chickpeas and greens, 73

    string beans with bacon and, 46

    stuffed with squid salad, 35

    sun-dried, leek, and goat cheese frittata, 117

    tapenade, pasta with, 149

    –white bean sauce, mussels in, 92

    zucchini with chorizo and, 46

tomato paste, 10

tostadas:

    black bean, 43

    Italian, 173

trout, smoked, spinach salad with apples and, 166

truffled arugula prosciutto salad, poached eggs and,
    166

tuna, 12

    -anchovy sandwich, 40

    and bean salad, 170

    black and blue, 47

    pasta with Moroccan tapenade, 194

    with pineapple, cucumber, and avocado, 48

    salad niçoise, 165

    sandwich with fennel and tarragon, 79

    seared, with capers and tomatoes, 90

    tabouleh, 34

turkey:

    cutlets with walnuts and sage, 142

    and pear wrap with curried aioli, 81

turnip, cream soup, 74

udon noodles, 11

    with green tea broth, 161

    and miso soup with fresh shiitake mushrooms, 75

    with seafood and soy-lemon sauce, 197

uncomplicated recipes (list), 20–21

veal cutlets, pan-fried, 192

vegetables, 12, 13

    frozen, 14

    gazpacho, 31

    grilled, with quinoa, 47

    ketchup-braised tofu with, 174

    mixed, stir-fried with ginger, 85

    mixed, soup, 118

    root, stir-fry, 83

    spiced, with raisins, 84

    see also specific vegetables

vermicelli, 11

very good burger, 58

Vietnamese caramelized grilled pork, 188

Vietnamese noodle soup with beef, 164

Vietnamese rice noodle salad with crab, 126

vinegars, 10

vodka sauce, penne with, 106

walnuts:

    -coated fish, 88

    -miso vinaigrette, broiled eggplant with, 39

    pesto, pasta with, 150

    snap peas with Roquefort and, 175

    turkey cutlets with sage and, 142

warm milk toast, 152

water, 10

watermelon:

    and feta salad, 38

    and shrimp skewers, grilled, 50

weekend brunch menu, 209

weeknight dinner party menu, 203

West Indian pork kebabs, 99

wheat, cracked, 10

whipped grapefruit cream with chocolate drizzle, 154

white beans:

    braised cabbage with Spanish chorizo and beans, 130

    mash, grilled lamb steak and, 102

    quick cassoulet, 122

    and salmon sandwich, 127

    and spinach soup, 162

    stew, 119

    Swiss chard with pancetta and, 45

    toasts, 79

    –tomato sauce, mussels in, 92

    see also beans, specific beans

white salad, 125

wine:

    chicken piccata, 141

    chicken poached in port, 141

    coq au vin, 138

    red,-braised lamb chops, 147

    white, and apple cider slushy, 109

    white, mussels in garlic and, 133

    white, seared scallops with chile and, 181

Worcestershire sauce, 10

    grilled pork skewers with, 56

wraps, see sandwiches

yogurt, 13

    lemony sauce, grilled lamb chops with, 59

    sauce, Moroccan spiced chicken with, 188

zucchini:

    braised fish with, 88

    and chickpea tagine, 120

    and dill soup, 31

    and garlic fusilli with pistachios, 108

    with tomatoes and chorizo, 46

zuppa di pane (bread soup), 119